TWAYNE'S WORLD AUTHORS SERIES

A Survey of the World's Literature

INDIA

Bhartṛhari

TWAS 403

BHARTṚHARI

By HAROLD G. COWARD

The University of Calgary

TWAYNE PUBLISHERS

A DIVISION OF G. K. HALL & CO., BOSTON

First Printing

Library of Congress Cataloging in Publication Data

Coward, Harold G
Bhartṛhari.

(Twayne's world author series ; TWAS 403 : India)
Bibliography: 139 - 40.
Includes index.
1. Bhartṛhari.
PK3791.B29C6 891'.2'1 [B] 76-8940
ISBN 0-8057-6243-4

MANUFACTURED IN THE UNITED STATES OF AMERICA

To Rachel

Contents

About the Author

Harold G. Coward is Head of the Department of Religious Studies at the University of Calgary, Calgary, Alberta, Canada. He holds a Ph.D. in Indian Philosophy and Religion from McMaster University, and an M.A. in Psychology from the University of Alberta. In 1972 the author was a visiting research scholar at Banaras Hindu University, Varanasi, India, where he studied with Professor T. R. V. Murti. Professor Coward is on the national executive of the Canadian Society for the Study of Religion.

The author's published essays and reviews have appeared in the *Journal for the Scientific Study of Religion*, *Studies in Religion*, *The Proceedings of the American Academy of Religion* and *The Chelsea Journal*. In September 1976 he organized "The Calgary Mysticism Conference" which examined the nature of mysticism in its Eastern, Western and North American Indian forms. His current major research interests include: a critical relating of Bhartṛhari to contemporary Western biblical criticism, a comparative study of Tamil and Hebrew devotional poetry; and an examination of Jungian psychology in relation to Eastern thought.

Preface

Several years ago I was working as a cognitive psychologist on a project aimed at founding a new field of psychological research — "epistemological psychology," as it has been named. The general question asked was "How does one know?" both philosophically and psychologically. The specific question that has continued to fascinate me is "How do we know via language?" How do the ordinary words of everyday conversation, the poetic words of aesthetic experience, and the special words of scriptural revelation convey their meaning, their truth to us? In Western philosophy, psychology, and theology, I found this study very difficult to pursue because of the academic alienation that exists among these disciplines. In traditional Indian thought, however, I found that there were no brick walls between disciplines and that the question of how language conveys and reveals word meanings had a long and respected academic parentage.

In my study of Indian thought, I was guided by my former teacher, Professor T. R. V. Murti, back to the ancient debate between Kumārila Bhaṭṭa the Mīmāṁsaka, and Bhartṛhari, the great Grammarian. I found myself particularly drawn to Bhartṛhari's thinking because it spanned the diverse disciplines of philosophy, psychology, and theology, and because it has been debated right up to the present day. In addition it seemed to relate in a creative way both to very ancient concepts of language, such as Plato's notion of externally existing ideas, and to some very modern notions, such as Chomsky's theory of innate universal grammatical structures. Although Bhartṛhari lived in India many centuries ago, his writing has a universal appeal that spans the years and bridges the gulf between East and West. This very timelessness in conjunction with universality strongly suggests that Bhartṛhari as grammarian, metaphysician, and poet has come close to revealing the fundamental nature of consciousness itself.

The *Vākyapadīya*, Bhartṛhari's great work on language and metaphysics, is technical Indian Sanskrit philosophy at its best. I have done my best to make it understandable to the beginning English reader, but have also included in the text the key Sanskrit terms (with translations) since some of these concepts are not always clearly expressible in English. A glossary of Sanskrit terms is provided. All quotations from and references to the *Vākyapadīya* are based upon K. A. Subramania Iyer's excellent English translation. It should be noted, however, that his numbering of verses is sometimes different from the usual numbering. Bhartṛhari's philosophy of language, and the Yoga psychology assumed, is complex and may prove to be heavy going for those not philosophically inclined. Readers more interested in Bhartṛhari's poetry or contribution to Indian aesthetics can safely omit the more difficult parts of Chapters 2 and 3 and go on to Chapter 4. In Chapters 4 and 5, brief summaries or reviews of Bhartṛhari's philosophy and psychology have been included.

I owe sincere thanks to many individuals: to Dr. M. L. Sharma, editor of this series, for patiently guiding me in the writing of this book; and to my colleague Dr. Inder Kher, for encouraging me to extend my study of Bhartṛhari so as to include his aesthetics and poetry. Dr. J. G. Arapura helped me to untangle some of the difficulties encountered in the Yoga interpretation of Bhartṛhari. My deepest debt, however, is to Dr. T. R. V. Murti, who introduced me to Bhartṛhari and spent many long hours patiently reading these ancient Indian texts with me.

HAROLD G. COWARD

The University of Calgary
October, 1975

Chronology

Although Bhartṛhari is a renowned author in Sanskrit literature and philosophy, exact details about his life and dates are not fully known. Tradition says that he was a king, perhaps a brother of either Vikramāditya or Sūdraka, who gave up his worldly life and became a *sannyāsin*, or forest dweller. Bhartṛhari's life has been dramatized by Harihara in his *Bhartṛharinirveda*. In this story Bhartṛhari is portrayed as a student of Gorakṣanātha, from whom he learns Yoga and renounces the world.[1] Much of the evidence regarding Bhartṛhari's date comes from Buddhist sources.[2] I-tsing, the Chinese Buddhist who studied at the Nālundā monastery, reports that Bhartṛhari died forty years earlier. This would put Bhartṛhari's death at either ca. A.D. 650 (if the forty years is calculated from I-tsing's writing of his travels in India) or ca. A.D. 630 (if the forty years is calculated from the beginning of I-tsing's stay at Nālundā). However, I-tsing also says that Bhartṛhari was a contemporary of Dharmapāla, whose dates are well known as A.D. 530–561, which makes I-tsing's dating self-contradictory and unacceptable.[3] More reliable evidence has come from a series of scholars who have uncovered quotations from Bhartṛhari's works in Tibetan translations of Buddhist texts such as Diṅnāga's *Pramāṇasamuccaya*. These show that Bhartṛhari must have either lived before or been a contemporary of Diṅnāga, whose dates are usually taken as ca. A.D. 470–550. Further indications from these Tibetan Buddhist translations and from a sixth-century Jaina writer, Siṃhasūrigaṇi, suggest that Bhartṛhari studied under the great grammarian of his day, Vasurāta, and that Vasurāta was a Brahmin and a brother-in-law of Balāditya, a pupil of the great Buddhist scholar Vasubandhu (ca. A.D. 400).[4] These plus other considerations lead to the current consensus among scholars that Bhartṛhari should be dated ca. A.D. 450-500.[5] This date, however, may still be open to further change. While the sequence of these writers seems fairly well established (i.e., Vasubandhu–Vasurāta–Bhartṛhari–Diṅnāga), the exact date assigned to each may have to be adjusted as new evidence is encountered.

With this difficulty in establishing Bhartṛhari's own dates, it is not surprising that nothing further can be said about the dates of his works or their order of appearance. Consequently, the works usually attributed to Bhartṛhari are simply listed as follows:

Works Attributed to Bhartṛhari[6]

1. *Mahābhāṣyaṭīkā:* only a fragment still exists of the commentary on the *Mahābhāṣya* of Patañjali.
2. *Vākyapadīya*, Chapters I, II, III: Bhartṛhari's great work on the Sanskrit philosophy of language.
3. *Vṛtti* on *Vākyapadīya* I and II: a commentary explaining the above work.
4. *Śabdadhātusamīkṣā:* a work that is currently lost.
5. *Śatakas* on *Nīti*, *Śṛṅgāra*, and *Vairāgya:* well-known Sanskrit poems on politics, passionate love, and renunciation.

CHAPTER 1

Bhartṛhari in His Own Day

I *India in the Time of Bhartṛhari*

BHARTṚHARI lived in the golden age of Indian philosophy, literature, art, and architecture. Northern India was politically unified and ruled by the Guptas, who encouraged scholarship and the arts. Skandagupta was likely ruler during much of Bhartṛhari's lifetime.[1] The government was mild, crime was rare, and the kings, although religiously tolerant, were Hindus. Sanskrit culture flourished under royal encouragement, and just before the time of Bhartṛhari, Kālidāsa had produced his great poetry at the court of Chandragupta II. Chinese pilgrims came to the sacred places of Buddhism and have left their travel diaries as eyewitness accounts of the age.[2] The people of the period are described as being numerous and happy. Rest houses were set up along the roadsides where travelers could obtain beds, food, and drink. Scholarly education was encouraged with beautiful teaching monasteries located in the major centers. In addition there were two large and internationally known universities located at Valabhī and Nālundā. The ruins of the latter have been excavated and, even today, are most impressive. I-tsing, the Chinese scholar, compared these two institutions to the best educational institutions of China, and Nālundā is considered to be the second university in the world — after Plato's academy in Athens. The Chinese pilgrims report that the people were of a hasty temperament but most moral in behavior. Vegetarian food was common, with onions and garlic being used only by the foreigners or the lower classes. The use of alcohol was looked down upon. Household utensils were earthenware, brass, or copper. Gold and silver were used for coinage in an economy that seemed to provide a good life for almost all social classes.

The position of women during Bhartṛhari's time had many interesting features. There was little seclusion and the women evidently still had a dominant role in the selection of their husbands. Among the upper-class women, higher education, including knowledge of Sanskrit and the fine arts, was the norm. Poetesses such as Śilabhaṭṭārikā achieved distinction. Women often shared in the administration of an area (e.g., in Kashmir, Orissa, and Andhra, queens were rulers, and women also acted as provincial governors and village heads) as well as taking part in the public scholarly debates on matters of religion, philosophy, and law.[3]

II *The Nature of Sanskrit Language and Literature*

Since all of Bhartṛhari's writing, both his poetry and his scholarly treatises, is in classical Sanskrit, it is essential that the modern reader have some sense of that language — its thought forms, its strengths and limitations. Daniel Ingalls has made some helpful observations in this regard. "The word Sanskrit originally meant 'refined' or 'perfected.' Accordingly, the Sanskrit language, to use the term correctly, is that language which was perfected in India by the great grammarians, especially by Pāṇini and Patañjali."[4] Literature in this medium begins before the time of Christ, but after the Vedic period, and continues to the Moslem invasion in A.D. 1200. Although Sanskrit continues after that date, it becomes more the language of the scholarly few, and is increasingly superseded by the popular languages of the masses, for example, Hindi.

Sanskrit differs from most other languages, including classical Latin and Greek, in one important respect — its artificiality, or remoteness from the emotional responses of everyday life. Sanskrit was seldom the common language of family life, and therefore lacks the strong feeling referents of everyday languages such as English or Bengali. But the opposite side of this limitation is that in Sanskrit there are vast numbers of synonyms that can be easily interchanged due to the lack of strong feeling attachments between the words and their concrete usage in ordinary life. Sanskrit possesses an intellectual quality that allows the same sentence to be expressed in ten or more different ways. Although each of these sentences would have a different formal construction (by the use of different word orders, or compound words, or various verb tenses, etc.), they would be interchangeable in terms of their evocative emotional power. This is quite different from ordinary languages where the everyday usage results in more definite emotional attachment of each word and therefore less flexibility.

It is for this reason that Sanskrit literature can maintain a very rigid set of complicated poetic or prose forms. Each verse must be four lines long and must follow one of the many recognized rhythmic patterns. Consequently Sanskrit is, by definition, very rational and orderly. It is the language of the scholars. Ingalls illustrates this point by quoting the Sanskrit poet Yogeśvara:

> Now the great cloud-cat
> darting out his lightning tongue
> licks the creamy moon
> from the saucepan of the sky

as against a passage using similar ideas in the contemporary English poetry of T. S. Eliot:

> The yellow fog that rubs its back upon the windowpanes
> The yellow smoke that rubs its muzzle on the windowpanes,
> Licked its tongue into the corners of the evening,
> Lingered upon the pools that stand in drains. . . .

Whereas in Sanskrit the effect is gained by the orderly, rational delineation of the metaphor through analogy, in English Eliot gets his effect from the juxtaposition of "licked its tongue into the corners" (as a cat might do with his bowl) with "of the evening," which is thoroughly irrational but evocative of complex associations and emotions.[5] Sanskrit, therefore, is by nature more orderly and intellectual than everyday spoken languages such as English. But this does not imply that Sanskrit has no power of evocation — just that the techniques used are more defined in terms of form, but given great scope by the vast numbers of synonyms and differing word orders possible.

It is because of this intellectual and formal nature that Sanskrit, if spoken to an audience not knowledgeable of its conventions, requires a commentary many times longer than the original verse to bring out the intended meaning. This is equally true for poetry, such as Bhartṛhari's *Śatakas,* and philosophical discourses, such as Bhartṛhari's *Vākyapadīya.* The discourse will first take the technical form of a *sūtra,* in which the meaning is presented in a nutshell, as it were. The commentaries then develop and explain the meaning with illustrations. This is all very intellectual, yet in spite of this evident intellectuality the further uniqueness of Sanskrit, in both poetry and prose, is that usually the implicit goal is to transcend the level of the intellect, and to reach the higher realm of spirituality and intuitional truth.

During the Gupta age Sanskrit poetry and philosophy were given a high place in the royal courts. It was a time of great literary activity producing great Sanskrit writers such as the poet and dramatist Kālidāsa and the philosopher Diṅnāga. Kālidāsa's own writings indicate that poetry, drama, art, and music were all practiced with intensity, and that an adequate education required knowledge and skill in the performance of these arts. It is evident that poetry and music were important subjects in a king's syllabus of study. Of the Gupta rulers, Samudra Gupta apparently produced excellent poetry and Skanda Gupta is said to have had good ability in music.[6] According to tradition Bhartṛhari himself came from just such a royal household, being the elder brother of King Vikramāditya who ruled at Ujjain.[7]

III *Bhartṛhari and the Religion of His Day*

It has been said of the Gupta period that although art and literary activity were respected for their aesthetic value, it was the religious aspect that really dominated all activity. This is an insight that any modern reader must become sensitive to if he is to be able to comprehend life as Bhartṛhari experienced it. And nothing less than this "putting of oneself in the other person's shoes" will result in any real understanding of the subject. This is especially true with regard to the radically different way that religion was, and in some places still is, conceived in the Indian tradition. All activity was interpreted as being a form of religious self-realization. As Krishnamoorthy puts it:

> The genius of India is such that even the most mundane activity is naturally viewed as religious. This is a country where cooking, eating, bathing and sleeping can be regarded as religious. Cutting across the infinite varieties of religious sects and forms of worship, there is a fundamental unity of common approach to all which is generally missed by the Westerner. In this widest sense, dance and drama, music and painting, are so many ways of divine worship.[8]

This does not mean that all artistic and literary activity was put under the thumb of religious dogma. What it does mean is that artists and writers in India "were religious in their personal lives, and took their vocation very seriously, so seriously that they deemed their art work to be on a par with the hardest disciplines like *yoga*."[9] Writing a textbook on grammar, composing a poem or a metaphysical system were each done as a discipline or practice for spiritual self-realization (*sādhanā*).[10]

In Bhartṛhari's day, the permeation of the whole culture by Hindu religion was at its peak. It was when the Brāhmanical religion of the Vedas surged past its rivals, the Buddhists and the Jains, to its full flowering. But whereas the popular Hindu religion of the day, perhaps following the lead of the Buddhists, was turning more and more to the image worship that came to characterize the religion of the epics and Puranas,[11] Bhartṛhari returned to the Vedas and Upaniṣads in true conservative fashion. Rather than finding Brahman in popular images, he experienced the Divine in the Vedic words themselves. This is consistent with the teaching of the Vedas. In the *Ṛg Veda* several hymns are devoted to inspired speech *(vāk)* and the same trends are continued in the Brāhmaṇas and the Upaniṣads.[12] Speech is described as the creation of the gods.[13] It permeates all creation.[14] But the Brāhmanical religious tradition, within which Bhartṛhari lived, went even further in identifying speech or language with the Divine. The *Ṛg Veda* states that there are as many words as there are manifestations of Brahman.[15] Even in the more recent Hindu scriptures, the Aranyakas and Upaniṣads, there is a continued equating of speech and Brahman. "The whole of Speech is Brahman."[16]

In this respect there seem to be close parallels between the Brāhmanical view that the Veda and Brahman are one, and the viewpoint expressed in Christian Scripture at the beginning of the Gospel according to Saint John, "In the beginning was the Word, and the Word was with God, and the Word was God." Both the Christian and the Brāhmanical viewpoints seem to agree that speech and the Divine coexist. But there are significant differences that must be carefully noted. Whereas the Christian Scripture conceives of an absolute beginning of order when God speaks and through his speaking creates,[17] the Brāhmanical view, shared by Bhartṛhari, believed in a cyclic view of creation with no absolute beginning. There may be beginning points for each cycle of creation, but there is no first cycle. The whole of the cosmos has constantly been going on through cycles of creation-dissolution, creation-dissolution . . . beginninglessly. At the dissolution of each cycle a seed or trace *(saṁskāra)* is left behind out of which the next cycle arises. It is an agricultural image of seed–flower–seed. . . .

The significant thing to note in relation to Bhartṛhari is that Brāhmanical religion describes the nature of the seed, from which each cycle of creation bursts forth, as "Divine Word." Various symbols are used to indicate the divine nature of speech and its evolution to form each cycle of creation. Professor Murti puts it well when he says, "The Brāhmanical tradition stemming from the Veda takes language as of divine origin *(Daivī Vāk)*, as Spirit descending and embodying itself in phenomena, assuming various guises and disclosing its real nature to the sensitive soul."[18] The "sensitive soul," in Brāhmanical religion, was the seer, or *ṛṣi* — who has purged himself of ignorance, rendering his consciousness transparent to the Divine Word. The *ṛṣi* was not the individual composer of the Vedic hymn, but rather the seer *(draṣṭā)* of an eternal impersonal truth. As Aurobindo puts it, the language of the Veda is "a rhythm not composed by the intellect but heard, a divine Word that came vibrating out of the Infinite to the inner audience of the man who had previously made himself fit for the impersonal knowledge."[19] The *ṛṣi*'s initial vision is said to be of the Veda as one, as a whole, the entirety of Brahman. This is represented in the *Māṅḍūkya Upaniṣad* by the *mantra* AUM, which includes within itself the three levels of ordinary consciousness — waking, dreaming, and deep sleep — yet also reaches out beyond to the transcendent where the sound itself comes to an end.[20] Brahman, which is said to be speech, is also said to be AUM.[21]

If, as Brāhmanical religion maintains, all of this is true, the question logically arises as to how this one Veda became split into the four separate Vedas *(Ṛg, Yajur, Sāma,* and *Atharva)*, which had become authoritative scripture long before Bhartṛhari. Why does not everyone have the same unitary divine vision as the original *ṛṣis*? The answer to this question, as commonly accepted in Bhartṛhari's time, runs as follows. The handing down of the one Veda in its four different forms (each with its various recensions or schools) occurred as a result of the decreasing capacity of man. This decreasing capacity in the form of increasing ignorance so obscured men's minds that they could no longer intuitively grasp the Veda as one, as the *ṛṣis* had done. Out of their concern for such men, the *ṛṣis* attempted to verbalize their vision in a form that would remove obscuring ignorance from the mind of the ordinary mortal so that he too could experience the divine vision that was eternally before him. And just as a medical specialist who knows the functioning of the human body as a total organism must begin by teaching his student of the many subsystems (nervous system, circulatory system, etc.) until finally the student, like his teacher, can see the unified functioning of the whole, so also the *ṛṣis* had to break down the unity of the Vedas into subparts, namely, the four Vedas with their various hymns and commentaries, as teaching aids to help the student discard the obscuring veil of his own ignorance and reach that same clear unitary vision of the Veda from which his teacher, the *ṛṣi*, had started.

From this perspective it is clear that the written and spoken scriptures are not the ultimate truth in itself. But the Vedas, uttered by the *ṛṣis*, serve the necessary and authoritative function of enabling one to "see" the ultimate Divine Word through its various penultimate verbalizations. As each cycle of creation progresses, the amount of obscuration veiling the visioning power of one's mind[22] is thought to increase, thus requiring more and more detailed commentaries from the teachers *(gurus)* so as to render the original verbalizations of Veda understandable. Consequently, the size of the *śāstra*, or authoritative teaching, increases as time goes on. As a particular creation cycle comes to its end *(pralaya)*, the veiling ignorance has become so dense as to almost completely shroud the revealing power of the original Vedas. The commentaries accumulated over the years themselves become such a maze of intricate reasoning that, for all but the exceptional few, they too become part of the obscuring ignorance. This does not mean, however, that the Vedic revelation has been forever lost, but only that it awaits the dissolution of the present cosmic cycle into its primal seed state so that a new cycle, in which the same eternal Veda may be seen afresh, can arise. The Veda, then, is one at the time of creation, but is verbalized in its diverse forms of *Ṛg*, *Sāma*, *Yajur*, and *Atharva* with appended commentaries because of the increasing ignorance of men, and again becomes one at the time of dissolution.

This is the accepted Brāhmanical viewpoint of Bhartṛhari's day, and, as chapter one of his *Vākyapadīya* makes clear, it is a viewpoint Bhartṛhari fully accepts. It is on the basis of this orthodox Hindu view of the cosmos that Bhartṛhari develops his philosophy of language and literary criticism. Understood within this context, Bhartṛhari's poetry, his metaphysics, and even his study of grammar are all seen to have a religious purpose. Expertise in Sanskrit grammar, for example, is not an end in itself, but enables one to more clearly hear the Sanskrit of the Veda, thus enhancing its revealing power within one's mind. For Bhartṛhari all of his literary activity was done as a discipline for spiritual self-realization. Directly it benefited him, but, in addition, it was conceived as a help to others — students who would seriously adopt Bhartṛhari as their *guru*. In this way Bhartṛhari followed in the tradition of the original *ṛṣis*, whose only purpose was to use the power of language to reveal that

Divine Word *(Śabdabrahman)* already present within the consciousness of everyone. Such revelation enabled one to transcend the suffering and bondage of this world *(karma-saṃsāra)* and achieve release of freedom from ignorance *(mokṣa)*.

IV *Bhartṛhari and the Metaphysics of His Day*

By the time of Bhartṛhari, classical Indian philosophy was well developed. As previously mentioned, the educational standard among the upper class was high. India possessed educational institutions that compared favorably with the best universities of Greece and the finest schools of China. Scholarship was highly valued and each king prided himself in the scholars he could attach to his court. Rather than the limelight of the civilization being focused upon sporting events (today's accepted practice), the clashing of wits as a scholar from one court or school debated with another was what grasped the attention of the people. Instead of six-figure prizes being offered to professional athletes, it was the scholar who received the king's purse of gold after defeating his colleagues on a fine point of scholastic debate. It was within this context that Bhartṛhari developed and presented his own thinking. Throughout the *Vākyapadīya* he states his own view by comparing it with the contrasting views of his day. Consequently, for Bhartṛhari's thinking to be understood, some knowledge of the lively metaphysical background of his own day is required — especially the positions taken by the various schools on the nature and function of language.

At the time of Bhartṛhari, Indian metaphysics was divided into orthodox (those who accepted the Vedas) and heterodox (those who rejected the Vedas) schools. The latter included the Jainas, Buddhists, and Cārvākas. The former included the Sāṅkhya, Yoga, Nyāya, Vaiśeṣika, Mīmāṁsā, and Vedānta. All of these schools accepted as a basic premise the scholastic Indian conception of knowledge as *pramā*. In Sanskrit the word *jñāna* stands for all kinds of cognition irrespective of the question of truth and falsehood, whereas the word *pramā* is used to designate only a true cognition *(yathartha-jñāna)* as distinct from a false one *(mithyā-jñāna)*. A true way of knowing, therefore, is called a *pramāṇa*.[23] Much of the argument among the various schools was over the question of how many *pramāṇas*, or valid ways of knowing, exist. Among the orthodox schools of the Brāhmanical tradition, the Sāṅkhya and the Yoga schools accept three *pramāṇas:* perception, inference, and the revelatory power of words *(śabda pramāṇa)*.[24] The Bhaṭṭa Mīmāṁsā defines six *pramāṇas: pratyakṣa*, or perception; *anumāna*, or inference; *śabda; upamana*, or analogy; *arthāpatti*, or presumption; and *abhāva*, or nonapprehension.[25] The same six *pramāṇas* are also stated by Vedānta.[26] Of course, there are many differences of definition regarding a specific *pramāṇa* among the schools. Since Bhartṛhari's concern is with the revelatory power of words, this discussion of his metaphysical context will focus only on the *śabda pramāṇa* and briefly examine the various interpretations offered by the abovementioned schools.

As noted previously, Indian speculations on the revelatory power of speech of *śabda pramāṇa* are already present in the Vedic hymns, and the same line of thought can be found continuing in the Brāhmaṇas and the Upaniṣads. Patañjali, in his *Mahābhāṣya*, comments on these earlier ideas establishing the basic formulations for a philosophy of language. These "seed" formulations are given further development by both the Mīmāṁsā and Bhartṛhari's Grammar school. Although these schools differ with regard to the exact way in which words reveal meaning, they both hold that the capacity of words to denote objects is inherent and given (with the exception of technical words and proper names). In the case of objects such as table or chair, experience is necessary to enable one to use the denotative word correctly, but the capacity of a word to signify a particular referent is intrinsic in it. In the case of words symbolizing supersensuous reality, such as "Brahman," we need not have seen the object or heard the word before to be able to understand its significance. Although perception, inference, comparison, and, in the case of the Bhaṭṭa Mīmāṁsā and Vedānta, postulation and negation, may give valid indications as to the nature of reality, it is only through the revelatory power of words *(śabda)* that ultimate knowledge of reality can be realized. While this high interpretation of *śabda* is the one that is developed by Bhartṛhari, it is in contrast with the evaluation of *śabda* by other schools of his day.

The Sāṅkhya school accepts *śabda* and defines it as authoritative statements arising from persons worthy of being believed and resulting in knowledge unattainable through perception or inference. Sāṅkhya scholars distinguish two qualities of word revelation: (1) special knowledge of supersensuous realities, which the Vedas alone can give, and (2) the general knowledge contained in the testimony of ordinary trustworthy persons.[27] Thus all language, when correctly spoken and understood, is taken as removing the veil of human ignorance *(avidyā)* and revealing knowledge of reality. In modern terminology, this would be described as "general revelation" in that the whole of language is seen as pregnant with divine meaning. It is distinct from, but establishes the basis for, the more theological conceptions of "special revelation."[28] Although Sāṅkhya formally admits *śabda* as an independent *pramāṇa,* it is inference that is really the chief way of knowing. The attitude of this school would seem to be to keep Vedic *śabda* handy to fall back on when inference and perception fail. In this respect it is somewhat akin to the modern attitude that consigns religion to the gaps that science has not yet filled in.

The Yoga school starts from a basic acceptance of Sāṅkhya theory, but evolves a much stronger conception of scriptural words. Perhaps the most noticeable difference between the Yoga and Sāṅkhya schools is the high place accorded to Īśvara, the Lord, by the former. And in the Yoga view, it is the Divine Word of the scripture in its transcendental essence that makes up the pure consciousness of Īśvara. Patañjali, the great Yoga teacher who likely lived in the same era as Bhartṛhari, elucidates this conception of Īśvara by emphasizing that in Īśvara the seed of omniscience is present in its utmost excellence. By inference it is shown that our process of knowing the supersensuous as it arises out of the past, future, or present, either collectively or individually, is possible only through the scriptual words — the verbalization of Īśvara's omniscience, which he has given to us only because of his compassion. This same Īśvara, in his omniscience, is the *guru* of the ancient *ṛṣis,* with whom he differs in that they are limited by time while he is not.

There is one word that when spoken connotes Īśvara with all his power for omniscience. That is the sacred syllable AUM. In his commentary on this *sūtra* Vyāsa raises many thorny questions regarding the nature of language. In answer to the question of whether the relationship between the word and the meaning signified is conventional or inherent, it is stated that the relationship is inherent and self-manifesting. The conventional activity of Īśvara is only for the purpose of manifesting this meaning, which is already inherently existing. In other creations, too, this same inherent relation between the word and its meaning existed. According to the Yoga school, Īśvara or God repeatedly re-creates this same convention in each new creation — it is in this sense that the scriptural words are said to be eternal.[29] This Yoga viewpoint has been described in some detail because it is a position that seems either to be very similar to that of Bhartṛhari or to have strongly influenced him.

The teachings of the Mīmāṁsā school are also in some ways very close to Bhartṛhari, yet in other ways he argues against them most strongly. Mīmāṁsā maintains that *śabda pramāṇa* is a valid and independent means of knowledge of the supersensuous. *Śabda* (which here stands for the Vedic word) is the chief *pramāṇa* for Mīmāṁsā, since it is the sole means for knowing injunctions and prohibitions *(dharma)*. The word, its meaning or denotation, and the relationship between these two are all judged to be inborn, eternal, and therefore not subject to creation by any person (e.g., God). When words come from human sources, there are many reasons why the validity or truth of the words may well be doubtful (trustworthiness of the speaker, his source of information, etc.). But if a word does not come from a human source it is not open to such defects and there can be no doubt regarding its impersonal truth. Thus the Veda is held to be impersonal, eternal, and infallible with regard to all that is supersensuous.[30]

The Mīmāṁsā doctrine of the word as eternal, infallible, and impersonal has aroused much controversy. How, for example, can the word be held to be eternally unchanging when it is not always present in one's consciousness; when it seems to cease or grow silent and to require human effort for its production again; and when one hears the same word uttered in varying forms of dialect, accent, or loudness? Śabara, the great Mīmāṁsā teacher, replies to such questions by saying that what is brought about by human effort is only the making present or manifestation of the already existing word.[31] When the sound of the spoken word is no longer heard, this is not due to any destruction of the word itself; rather, it is a case of nonperception of the word, which remains eternally present. And when one thinks of the great variety of accents, dialects, and so on, that exist, it is evident that only on the assumption of an eternally existing and unchanging word could communication between individuals take place. Śabara concludes that all this reasoning only supports the Vedic texts, which speak of the word as eternal.[32]

On all of the above general principles, Bhartṛhari is in agreement. But on at least two issues there is marked disagreement. For Bhartṛhari the eternal word that is manifested in uttered speech is the meaning-whole of the word or sentence — to which he gives the technical name *sphoṭa*. For the Mīmāṁsā, in contrast, it is the component letter sounds (e.g., c-o-w) that exist eternally and that when cognized sequentially result in the word-unit (e.g., "cow"). For Bhartṛhari the psychological process involved is one of perceiving the whole word, or *sphoṭa,* with the sense organ of the mind — a mental intuition. The Mīmāṃsā scholars flatly reject such supersensuous intuition as nothing more than fantasy. As Śabara puts it,

> What happens is that each component letter, as it is uttered, leaves an impression behind, and what brings about the cognition of the denotation of the word is the *last component letter along with the impressions of each of the preceding component letters.* In actual experience, the composite word-unit is never found to be anything entirely different from the component letters; hence there can be no 'word' apart from the component letters.[33]

The Mīmāṁsā school vehemently opposed Bhartṛhari's teaching that the real word was an idea-whole over and above the uttered letter sounds, and which could be directly perceived by the mind. They opposed this view because it placed the basis for ultimate knowledge not at the level of spoken language (i.e., the phenomenal Veda), but at some inner mystical level that, according to Bhartṛhari, was the real word. The logical consequence of such a theory, as the Mīmāṁsā scholars clearly saw, was the removal of the eternal sounds of the spoken Veda as the firm foundation for all knowledge.

The Vedānta school, although not yet systematized by Śaṅkara (ca. A.D. 800), likely existed in some beginning fashion in Bhartṛhari's day. Although there are no extant writings from Vedānta scholars of the period under consideration, a good indication of their approach to *śabda pramāṇa* can perhaps be obtained by examining Śaṅkara's analysis of the same topic. As in the Mīmāṁsā, the Vedānta school holds that the word, its meaning, and the relationship between the two are eternal and therefore not subject to creation by any person. Vedānta also agrees that *śabda pramāṇa* is vitally important in that it enables one to achieve *mokṣa.*

The capacity of *śabda* to give such "saving knowledge" assumes both the immediate apprehension of the meanings of words in a sentence, and the ability to understand the purport of a sentence. The former requires the absence of ignorance or delusion that would obstruct the apprehension of the knowledge inherent in *śabda.* The understanding of the purport of a sentence requires both concentrated study and the application of inference as developed by the Mīmāṁsā school. The six characteristics of purport are: the harmony of the initial and concluding passages, repetition, novelty, fruitfulness, glorification by eulogistic passages or condemnation by deprecatory passages, and intelligibility in the light of reasoning. When the purport of a sentence is both uncontradicted by other *pramāṇas* and unknown through other *pramāṇas*, then that sentence is held to be *śabda pramāṇa*, or a valid verbal revelation.

From this viewpoint, a false statement results, not because of any inadequacy in the words themselves, but because the delusions or ignorance of the person speaking act as an obstacle that prevents the intrinsic truth of the words from being cognized. In the case of a reliable person's statement, however, there are no such obstacles present, and the inherent meaning of the word is clearly cognized by the listener. On this theoretical basis, if it can be shown that there are certain sentences lacking authors, then the knowledge they give will be free from error. Thus the thesis of the Brāhmanical schools that the Veda is authorless and eternal. In cases where some *mantra* is said to have been composed by a particular *ṛṣi*, this does not mean that the *ṛṣi* in question created the *mantra* but rather that the *ṛṣi* himself has been generated from the words of the Veda. In his commentary on the *Brahma Sūtra*, Śaṅkara says that at the (relative) beginning of each creation *(kalpa)*, God, who is self-illumined, creates Brahmā and delivers the Vedas to him in the same form as they existed in previous creations. With this power Brahmā then gives to all the *ṛṣis*, who had existed previously, their same names and their same vision of the Vedic *mantras*. Just as the various seasons of the year return in succession, so the same seers and Vedas appear again in each different creation cycle, so that the Vedas of the present are equal in name and form to those of the past.[34] It is in this way that Vedānta maintains the impersonality and eternality of the Veda, while at the same time suggesting that God is somehow the eternal omniscient author. The argument is similar to the one used by Yoga in explaining the eternal coexistence of Īśvara and the Veda. Referring to the *Chāndogya Upaniṣad* (4.15.1), Śaṅkara argues that the Veda itself states that it is but breath of the great Being. As easily as a man exhales, so God produced the Veda, as if in play. Due to its self-evident omniscience and omnipotence, nothing but Brahman can be inferred as its cause.

Śaṅkara has dwelt on this point at some length and in so doing highlights a fundamental disagreement with Bhartṛhari. Śaṅkara carefully distinguishes between "evolution of the world from Brahman" and "evolution of the world from *śabda*." Brahman, he maintains, is the material cause of the world while *śabda* is only an efficient cause.[35] For Bhartṛhari, as was previously noted, Brahman and *śabda* are coextensive. *Śabdabrahman* for Bhartṛhari is both material and efficient cause of creation.

Śaṅkara also argues with the Mīmāṁsā and against Bhartṛhari's notion that the word-meaning is a perception or intuition by the mind of a supersensuous *sphoṭa*, or idea. According to Śaṅkara, in his commentary on *Brahma Sūtra* I.3.28, only the individual letter sounds of a word are perceived, and these are combined through the inferential activity of the mind into a word aggregate. This leads to another important debate between the two schools, namely, the question of how error *(avidyā)* is overcome.

Since Bhartṛhari conceives of the complete and true word meaning being achieved via the process of perception, albeit mental perception, this allows for increasing degrees of clarity as one's mind positively approximates itself to the truth that is there shining forth but not yet clearly seen. Error is thus overcome by a gradual approximation to the given meaning whole, or *sphoṭa*. In Śaṅkara's view, however, since the attainment of word-meaning occurs by the inferential activity of the mind (in grouping together the individual letters into an aggregate), and since the inference *pramāṇa* is an all or nothing process, the error, if it is to be overcome, must be completely replaced all at once by either a new inferential construction of the mind or a superconscious intuition of Brahman.

This approach is well illustrated in Vedānta thought by the explanation of the process by which the *mahāvākyas*, or great criterion sentences of the Vedas, can bring one to the experience of *mokṣa*. These authoritative sentences will first be perceived as conveying only mediate or inferential knowledge, but as one undergoes the fourfold mental and moral discipline (i.e., discrimination between the eternal and noneternal, giving up desires for the enjoyment of the fruits of actions either here or hereafter, acquisition of powers of concentration and endurance, and ardent desire for liberation), these truths known from *śabda pramāṇa* attain immediacy *(aparokṣatva)*. This process is illustrated by the story of the ten persons who, having crossed a river, count themselves. Every time the counter forgets to count himself and finds only nine. They mourn the loss of their tenth comrade. The error is corrected by a passerby who counts all, and tells the counter, "You are the tenth." This mediate inferential knowledge from *śabda* afterward becomes immediate knowledge when, counting again and including himself, the counter comes to realize "I am the tenth." In a similar way the earnest seeker perceives from the *mahāvākyas* that Brahman is the one reality in all outer things and in the inner self, and achieves an immediate consciousness of "I am Brahman."

Once this revelation is achieved, maintains Śaṅkara, then *śabda* and the Veda will have been superseded, since *śabda* is meaningful only when one is in the bondage of *avidyā*.[36] Although it is the only *pramāṇa* by which the liberation of absolute truth may be achieved, *śabda*, even as the *mahāvākyas*, is ultimately seen to be a part of worldly phenomenal diversity *(māyā)*, which must be negated if the ultimate absolute unity of Brahman is to be realized.[37] The Mīmāṁsā refusal to accept any kind of *pratibhā*, or immediate intuition, was to guard against just such an outcome in which the Vedas could be considered transcendable.

In opposition to this high evaluation given language by Bhartṛhari and the Brāhmanical schools,[38] the heterodox scholars, especially the Materialists (Cārvākas) and Buddhists, viewed language as an arbitrary and conventional tool. The Cārvāka school rejects *śabda pramāṇa* as completely false and accepts only the *pramāṇa* of perception as producing true knowledge. Sacred scriptures, religious injunctions, and so forth, are all considered useless. Everything is held to be derived from material elements *(mahābhūta)*, which are judged to possess their own immanent life force *(svabhāva)*. Intelligence, thought, and words are all seen as derived from these elements. There is no God, no supernatural, no immortal soul, and the only aim of life is to get the maximum of pleasure.[39]

Śabda pramāṇa is rejected by the Cārvāka on the grounds that it must first be established by other verbal testimony resulting in an infinite regress unless at some point there is an appeal to direct sensory experience. In addition to this logical reason for rejection, Cārvāka also holds that *śabda* is unacceptable on epistemological grounds — that it is impossible for perceptual knowledge to be communicated. The argument offered here is that a man knows only what he perceives, and not what someone else says he has perceived.[40] In this view the only referents are material, and direct sensory perception of such material referents is the only valid knowledge of reality.

Whereas for the Cārvākas sense perception was the only valid knowledge and pleasure produced by sensation the only goal, Buddha taught that "sense knowledge is considered to be inextricably bound up with feeling and desire, and hence is to be eliminated as far as possible because by its nature it is a stumbling block to the ultimate aim of the Buddha, the elimination of craving through understanding of illumination."[41] For the early Buddhists intuition is the highest source of knowledge. This intuition *(prajñā)* is defined as "knowledge of things as they are in themselves as distinguished from what they appear to us."[42] Such knowledge is considered to be the only means to freedom or salvation. *Prajñā* is frequently conceived as an omniscient eye. Buddha, for example, was said to have gained such a divine eye on the memorable night of his overthrow of the demon Māra. Through it he saw the entire knowable reality as if it were reflected in a clear mirror. Only such knowledge gained through one's own experience of intuition is considered to be valid. Sense experiences, words, inferences, and so on, are worthwhile only as they help one to overcome the obstacles of ordinary experience, and achieve *prajñā* for oneself. But, in themselves, *śabda*, sense perception, inference, et cetera, cannot be considered to give knowledge.

It is for this reason that Buddha rejected the Brāhmanical claims as to the authority of the Veda and its status as *pramāṇa*. The Vedic *ṛṣis*, he claimed, had no direct personal knowledge of the truth of the Veda.[43] But, as was pointed out in the previous section of this chapter, such personal knowledge is precisely what was claimed by the *ṛṣis*. This contention of Buddha, therefore, was virtually a denial that the *ṛṣis* were competent persons whose testimony could be trusted. Aside from this, it seems clear that Buddha's intention was not to discredit all *śabda* as incapable of conveying truth, but to show that the truth or falsity of any statement is to be judged by factors other than its claim to be reliable report, self-evident, or authoritative revelation. As Jayatilleke puts it, Buddha's criticism "seems to presuppose that it is possible to determine the veracity of all the assertions by other means than that of revelation, etc., in so far as it is stated that what is accepted as reliable may prove in fact to be true or false."[44] In spite of the fact that his followers tended to make Buddha's words into the very kind of absolute authority he was rejecting, it seems clear that Buddha's view was that his own teachings and the path to freedom contained therein were only to be accepted *provisionally* by the disciple until found to be truth in his own direct experience *(prajñā)*.

In general, the thrust of the Buddhist criticism of the Brāhmanical viewpoint seems aimed more toward discrediting the unquestioning acceptance of a handed-down tradition than toward the rejection of *śabda* as having any possibility for truth bearing. Buddha is said to have compared the generations of Vedic teachers to a string of blind men clinging one behind the other in succession. Just because a succession of teachers or teaching is unbroken is no guarantee of its truth. It is perhaps partly in response to this criticism of the early Buddhists that the Mīmāṁsā school developed the *apauruṣeya* theory, which makes *śabda* impersonal, eternal, and therefore free from the corrupting influences of personality and ill-remembered transmission as alleged by the Buddhists. In addition to this there is the Vedānta claim that not only is *śabda apaureṣeya* but its truth is necessarily realizable by experience *(anubhava)* in this life if one is to achieve salvation. This further interpretation by Vedānta would seem to satisfy the requirements of Buddha for confirmation in intuition and at the same time safeguard the Brāhmanical claim that *śabda* (and Veda) is *pramāṇa*. Buddha's reply to this would likely be that while the study of the Vedas may lead to the intuition of truth, this is not necessarily so. One who does not hear the Veda but follows the path of moral living and inner concentration, as pioneered by Buddha, can have the intuition of truth in the absence of *śabda*.

It appears that sometime after the death of Buddha there was an authoritative collection of Buddha's teachings. But "authoritative" here refers to the fact that these are the authentic teachings (against which all other texts claiming to be Buddha's words must be compared), and not to any truth claim of the teachings themselves. The criterion for truth, as it was for the Cārvākas, is direct empirical perception. But where the Buddhists differ from the Cārvākas is that the range of empirical perception is extended into what is usually referred to as the extrasensory realm. And just as the Cārvāka will allow for knowledge to result from inductive inferences on the data of sensory perception, so the Buddhists claim knowledge on the basis of inductive inferences on the data of extrasensory perception. Such extrasensory perceptions are not considered to be miraculous but simply the normal result of the natural development of the mind until the state of *prajñā*, or pure intuition, is achieved. The difference between this and Bhartṛhari's view is that for Bhartṛhari such pure intuition is necessarily constituted by the intertwining of word and consciousness. Knowledge content does not come from the object itself, but from its root epistemological cause which is *Daivī Vāk*, the Divine Word.

In summarizing the above metaphysical discussion current in Bhartṛhari's day, the following main points are noted. Each of the different schools of thought had put forth its own view of language and criticized the views of others. Indian speculations on the nature of language began with the Veda. In the *Ṛg Veda* it is said that there are as many words as there are manifestations of Brahman. The Brāhmaṇas and Upaniṣads continue to equate *vāk* and Brahman. The Sāṅkhya, Yoga, Mīmāṁsā, Vedānta, and Grammar schools are not only loyal to this tradition but give further development to these early "seed" concepts, with the grammarian Bhartṛhari producing the *sphoṭa* theory.

Bhartṛhari's *sphoṭa* theory, along with the Mīmāṁsaka theory, holds that the revelatory power of words *(śabda)* is both divine in origin and the means by which the Divine may be known. This viewpoint is opposed by the Cārvākas, the Buddhists, the Vaiśeṣikas, and the Nyāyas, who hold language to be more or less conventional in nature. Just as we create names for our children or for scientific discoveries, and thereby initiate new conventions, so also the origination of all words should be understood. In this view all words are the result of convention. Both the Mīmāṁsakas and Bhartṛhari's Grammar school adopt the view that the relation between the uttered word and its transcendent meaning is preestablished. But these two schools differ as to what aspect of speech is the primary unit that is correlated to the meaning. For the Mīmāṁsakas it is the phoneme, or letter-sound (e.g., the "c" in "cow"), that is the basic given; for the grammarians it is the totality of the word or sentence (the whole idea being conveyed) that is prior.

Taken to its logical conclusion this latter view results in an ascending hierarchy of levels of speech. Since Bhartṛhari's logic is that "the whole is prior to the parts," this means that the word is subsumed by the sentence, the sentence by the paragraph, the paragraph by the chapter, the chapter by the book, and so on, until all speech is identified with Brahman. From this conclusion, Bhartṛhari also makes the following deduction: there is no cognition without the words.[45] This seems to agree with the contention of at least one modern linguist, Edward Sapir, that there is no thought without language.[46] As Professor T. R. V. Murti puts it, it is not that we have a thought and then look for a word with which to express it; or that we have a lonely word that we seek to connect with a thought. "Word and thought develop together, or rather they are the expressions of one deep spiritual impulse to know and to communicate."[47]

By keeping in mind the basic points of these sophisticated metaphysical arguments, which were current in Bhartṛhari's day, the modern reader will have a much better chance of understanding and evaluating the significance of Bhartṛhari's own thinking on language and aesthetics.

CHAPTER 2

The Vakyapadiya's *Theory of Language*

I *Introduction to the* Vākyapadīya's *Approach*

THE seventh-century Chinese pilgrim to India, I-tsing, reports in his diary that in the education curriculum of the day Bhartṛhari's *Vākyapadīya*, coming after mastery of Patañjali's *Mahābhāṣya*, was crowning work studied by the best and most serious students. Even in the great Buddhist University at Nālundā, the *Vākyapadīya* was studied alongside the eighteen schools of Buddhist philosophy.[1] As the histories of the period indicate, the Gupta age gave the highest place to the study of Sanskrit grammar and the knowledge that language in its purest form can bring. Bhartṛhari's *Vākyapadīya* was considered to have been the culminating work in this Sanskrit *Vyākaraṇa* or Grammar school tradition, a reputation it has maintained to the present day.

In common with other Sanskrit works of the period, the *Vākyapadīya* was written in the form of concise *kārikās* or verses requiring an interpretative commentary for their full understanding. This commentary was written either by the author or by someone very close to him. The *vṛtti*, or commenatry, on *Vākyapadīya* I and II seems to have been written by Bhartṛhari[2] and helps the reader to more fully understand the otherwise brief *kārikās*. Not all of the *Vākyapadīya* has survived the ravages of time. The first chapter, in which the metaphysical ideas concerning the concept of *Śabdabrahman* are put forth, is fairly complete and has been translated into English by K. A. Subramania Iyer. Although we have the *kārikās* for chapter two, which deals with the structure and meaning of sentences, the *vṛtti* is missing in many places. Chapter three, which deals with problems relating to words, may also have sections missing. Current scholarship is at work on these problems.[3] Lest the reader be misled into thinking that the work is merely academic metaphysics and linguistics, Bhartṛhari's stated purpose should be held clearly in mind. At the beginning of the *Vākyapadīya* Bhartṛhari states that the knowledge and correct use of words does two things: it brings about spiritual merit *(dharma)* and it results in the understanding of meaning *(pratyaya)*. And by the end of the *Vākyapadīya* it is clear that, not only could the spiritual merit of heaven *(svarga)* be attained, but one should adopt the further and final goal of *mokṣa* — studying grammar in order to attain union *(sāyuja)* with the great deity within, namely, *Śabdabrahman*. With this high goal in mind the basic ideas of the *Vākyapadīya* can now be examined.

In outlining the metaphysical background, it was pointed out that for the main Brāhmanical schools, language is both a valid source of knowledge and the means by which such knowledge may be communicated to others as verbal truth *(śabda pramāṇa)*. Emphasizing this latter function, Bhartṛhari's predecessors, the early grammarians Paṇini and Patañjali, describe *śabda* primarily in terms of the spoken sounds or "outer word." In the first verse of his *Mahābhāṣya*, Patañjali defines the word as "that on the utterance of which there is common understanding regarding objects *(saṁpratyaya)*."[4] This definition of *śabda* does not intend the identification of the word with the physiological production of speech. As Murti has pointed out, the distinction between word *(śabda)* and sound *(dhvani)* is basic to the understanding of language in all schools of Indian philosophy. To take the physical sound as the word is to confuse entities of two different orders, like the confusion of the soul with the body. "The word, like the soul, has a physical embodiment in the sound and is made manifest through the latter, but the conveyance of meaning is the function of the word; the sound only invokes the word."[5]

Now if the word, or *śabda*, is only manifested and not constituted by the vocal sounds, or *dhvani*, the question then arises as to the exact nature of this *śabda* which is manifested. We have seen, according to the heterodox schools, that just as we create names for our children and for scientific discoveries and so initiate new conventions, the origination of all words should be understood in a similar way. In this way of thinking all words are the result of convention. Where human convention is not allowable, the divine convention of God may be invoked — as is done by the Nyāya, for example. Against this view, Bhartṛhari supports the Brāhmanical schools, especially the Mīmāṁsā, in their contention that words and their relation with meaning are eternal, underived, and impersonal. The relation between *śabda* and its meaning is not an arbitrary convention established by either man or God or both. Not only is there no record of any such convention, but the very idea of "convention" itself presupposes language — the very thing claimed to be derived from convention. Murti makes the point quite clear: "To make conventions, words have to be used and understood by persons participating in the convention. This is clearly circular. Invoking God does not help either. How could God make known his intentions, his conventions between words and their respective meanings to persons who did not use language already?"[6]

It would seem, therefore, that language must be taken as having existed beginninglessly; or, as somehow being coeternal with God. As Murti suggests, the attempt to discover a temporal beginning of language may arise from a confusion of the *śabda*, or inner word, and *dhvani*, or spoken sounds. While speaking sounds, learning how to group sounds into syllables, and so on, may well be conventional, the fact of verbal communication necessitates the acceptance of *śabda* as a given that the learned spoken sounds manifest, but do not constitute.

Here the viewpoint of Bhartṛhari and the Brāhmanical tradition seems very similar to the Platonic concept of the universality and eternity of the idea. Whereas in Platonic doctrine the relation of the idea to the "copies" is described as the relation of the immutable to its several manifestations, here the word is the immutable, which is first perceived through its several physical manifestations. The word "cow," for example, is a word-form that is identical and immutable, although its physical manifestations may differ markedly with regard to accent, speed of speaking, place and time of utterance, and so forth. But Bhartṛhari goes further than just establishing the eternality of *śabda*. He identifies *śabda* with the Brahman — all words ultimately mean the Supreme Brahman. The meaning intended by this absolutistic claim is described as follows:

> . . . Brahman is the one object denoted by all words; and this one object has various differences imposed upon it according to each particular form; but the conventional variety of the differences produced by these illusory conditions is only the result of ignorance. Non-duality is the true state; but through the power of "concealment" [exercised by illusion] at the time of the conventional use of words a manifold expansion takes place.[7]

On this basis, knowledge of the meaning of words not only abolishes ignorance but also leads to the final bliss of identity with Brahman.

Another basic issue included in the language debate among the various schools is the question of whether *śabda* signifies its meaning through the universal or through the particular. Indian language speculation appears to contain a vast variety of views ranging from the extreme nominalism of the Buddhist to the realism of the Mīmāṁsā and the Nyāya. On this question the school of Grammar offers two views. In the *Vākyapadīya,* Bhartṛhari first makes clear that the real unit of language is the sentence, and that for pedagogical purposes words are abstracted from the sentence and ascribed a meaning. Thus the idea that words are divided into syllables and sentences into words is a convenient fiction. According to the one view suggested by the school of Grammar, the word-meaning is connoted by the universal. As Murti puts it, "The universal is primarily a Word-Form and by way of transference this is applied to the Idea-Universal."[8] The particulars are merely the appearances of the universal. For practical purposes we may speak of several universals, such as man, cow, horse, and so on; but in the final analysis there is only one ultimate universal-being, and it is this that all words mean.

This view is by its logic identical to the Advaita Vedānta position, which holds in all things for the nonduality of the real and the appearance and defines the relationship as a one-sided dependence upon the real. The other view suggested by the school of Grammar is that the meaning is to be found in the individual object the word denotes. Here substance or the substantive being of the particular is taken as the thing that remains permanent throughout the changes. Meaning in this view is denotation — the *that* of things. Ultimately, of course, there is still one indivisible being that is the meaning of all individual words. In this case the individuals are seen as appearances that exist through limitation *(upādhi)* of the one universal being.

But the most important issue for the school of Grammar is the question, "What constitutes the meaning-unit of language?" It is here that Bhartṛhari's *sphoṭa* theory is presented as a direct challenge to all the other positions reviewed above. In criticizing the Mīmāṁsā, Vedānta, and Nyāya view that the individual letters or words of a sentence generate the meaning, the grammarian points out that the letters of a word or the words in a sentence die away as soon as they are pronounced so that when we arrive at the last letter of a word or the last word of a sentence, the previous elements have all vanished. How then can the meaning of the whole word or sentence be cognized? If it is replied that memory holds the traces of the letters and words, this still does not help, since, as only one thing can be cognized at a time in our mind, the memory traces will only replay the serial presentation of the original parts and no whole meaning will be generated. Therefore, says the grammarian, since meaning is a single or unitary whole, so also its generating condition must likewise be a whole. On this assumption the *sphoṭa* theory is advanced — the idea that the word or sentence is an indivisible unity that is inherently given and engenders all meaning. The separate letters of a word or words of the sentence merely manifest the *sphoṭa*, or meaning-whole. In Mādhava's *Sarva-Darśana-Saṃgraha* the argument is put this way: ". . . as the letters cannot cause the cognition of the meaning, there must be a *sphoṭa* by means of which arises the knowledge of the meaning; and this *sphoṭa* is an eternal [inner] sound distinct from the letters and revealed by them, which causes the cognition of the meaning."[9]

II *Bhartṛhari's Definition of* Sphoṭa

For Bhartṛhari, the word or sentence when taken as an indivisible meaning-unit is the *sphoṭa*. The technical term *sphoṭa* is difficult to translate into English. Sometimes the word "symbol" is used for *sphoṭa* in the sense of its function as a linguistic sign. It has also been suggested that the original Greek conception of *logos* best conveys the meaning of *sphoṭa*. "The fact that *logos* stands for an idea as well as a word wonderfully approximates to the concept of *sphoṭa*."[10] The spoken sounds or printed letters of ordinary language are distinguished from the *sphoṭa* in that the former are merely the means by which the latter is revealed. The term *sphoṭa* is derived from the Sanskrit root *sphuṭ*, which means "to burst forth." In his Sanskrit-English dictionary, V. S. Apte defines *sphoṭa* as: (1) breaking forth, bursting or disclosure; and (2) the idea that bursts out or flashes on the mind when a sound is uttered.[11] The original conception of *sphoṭa* seems to go far back into the Vedic period of Indian thought when, as was shown in the previous chapter, *vāk*, or speech, was considered to be a manifestation of the all-pervading Brahman, and the *praṇava* (AUM) regarded as the primordial speech-sound from which all forms of *vāk* are supposed to have evolved. This sacred syllable is said to have flashed forth into the heart of Brahman, while he was absorbed in deep meditation, and to have given birth to the Vedas containing all knowledge. At the very beginning of the *Vākyapadīya*, Bhartṛhari restates these very teachings as the foundation for his thinking.[12] Just as the original unitary Veda has been handed down in many ways by the *ṛṣis* for the sake of communication, so also the unitary idea of *sphoṭa* is manifested as a series of uttered sounds for purposes of expression and communication.

Although Bhartṛhari may have modeled his concept of *sphoṭa* on the Vedic *praṇava*, his method of approach was strikingly different. Rather than just immersing himself in mystical meditation, he sets out to analyze the meanings of words and the means by which such word knowledge is manifested and communicated in ordinary experience. In his *Vākyapadīya*, Bhartṛhari states, "In the words which are expressive the learned discern two aspects: the one [the *sphoṭa*] is the cause of the real word [while] the other *[dhvani]* is used to convey the meaning."[13] These two aspects, although they may appear to be essentially different, are really identical. The apparent difference is seen to result from the various external manifestations of the single internal *sphoṭa*. The process is explained as follows. At first the word exists in the mind of the speaker as a unity, or *sphoṭa*. When he utters it, he produces a sequence of different sounds so that it appears to have differentiation. The listener, although first hearing a series of sounds, ultimately perceives the utterance as a unity — the same *sphoṭa* with which the speaker began — and it is then that the meaning is conveyed.[14]

For Bhartṛhari, the two aspects of word-sound *(dhvani)* and word-meaning *(artha)*, differentiated in the mind and yet integrated like two sides of the same coin, constitute the *sphoṭa*.[15] He emphasizes the meaning-bearing or revelatory function of this two-sided unity, the *sphoṭa*, which he maintains is eternal and given in nature. He generally describes one's cognition of the *sphoṭa* from the hearer's perspective. By a child learning a word, or by an adult on first hearing a word, the *sphoṭa* is usually at first cognized erroneously. Having failed to grasp the whole *sphoṭa*, the listener asks, "What did you say?" Through a series of erroneous cognitions, in response to the repeated vocalizations, of the word-sounds, there arises a progressively clearer cognition of the *sphoṭa*. Finally there is a completely clear cognition of the whole *sphoṭa* and its two-sided aspects, which Bhartṛhari describes as a case of special perception or intuition. The inital error has given place to truth in which the two aspects of word-sound and word-meaning have become completely identical in the unity of the *sphoṭa*.

Since the cognition of this final and *a priori sphoṭa* unity is held to be a case of perception (albeit supersensuous), various perceptual analogies are offered as examples. For instance, when the expert jeweler finally sees the genuineness of a precious stone after a continuous gaze at it consisting of a series of comparatively vague cognitions of it, it is a case of perception. Bhartṛhari claims that means of knowledge other than perception (e.g., inference) either reveal the object or do not reveal it at all. It is only perception where the object (in this case the word-meaning) is at first seen vaguely and then more and more clearly. While all of this is the process experienced by ordinary men, Bhartṛhari, along with most other Indian philosophers, allows that the great *ṛṣis* are able to cognize the complete unitary *sphoṭa* directly, without having to go through the process of repeated perception and error correction.

In his discussion, Bhartṛhari employs three technical terms: *śabda/sphoṭa, dhvani,* and *nāda.* By *śabda* and/or *sphoṭa,* he refers to that inner unity which conveys the meaning. The *dhvanis* are described as all-pervasive and imperceptible particles which, when amassed by the movement of the articulatory organs, become gross and perceptible sounds and are then called *nāda.* These *nādas* function to suggest the word, *sphoṭa* or *śabda.* And since these *nādas,* which are gross and audible, have division and sequence, it is naturally assumed that the suggested word also has parts, when in reality it is changeless and sequenceless. Bhartṛhari offers the illustrative example of reflection in water. Just as an object reflected in water may seem to have movement because of the movement of the water, similarily the word, or *sphoṭa,* takes on the properties of uttered speech (sequence, loudness or softness, accent, etc.) in which it is manifested.[16]

Perhaps one can best understand Bhartṛhari's notion of *sphoṭa* when it is illustrated in poetry. Take, for example, the following verse from T. S. Eliot's "Burnt Norton."

> Desire itself is movement
> Not in itself desirable;
> Love is itself unmoving,
> Only the cause and end of movement,
> Timeless, and undesiring
> Except in the aspect of time
> Caught in the form of limitation
> Between un-being and being.
> Sudden in a shaft of sunlight
> Even while the dust moves
> There rises the hidden laughter
> Of children in the foliage

Quick now, here, now, always —
Ridiculous the waste sad time
Stretching before and after.[17]

In this verse Eliot composes a variety of word-images that, when uttered, manifest in the hearer's consciousness an intuitive perception of eternal love. While the great *ṛṣi* or saint may perceive such eternal love directly in its full purity, ordinary human beings must begin with a variety of partial perceptions that gradually open the mind to a full experience of eternal love (the *sphoṭa*). Eliot, the poet, has intuited the *sphoṭa*, and skillfully, through his poetry, is attempting to produce that same intuition in the minds of his readers. Each of the images used evokes the *sphoṭa* of eternal love in the mind. With each new image the *sphoṭa* intuition achieves clearer definition, until it is sharply and fully revealed. Each of the poetic images is in itself an imperfect expression of the *sphoṭa*, but through them the full meaning and experience of eternal love is known. Chapter 4 will discuss how Bhartṛhari's analysis of language in terms of the *sphoṭa* theory has come to occupy a central place in the history of Indian aesthetics.

If one accepts Bhartṛhari's basic premise, namely, that the meaning-whole, or *sphoṭa*, is the fundamental unit of language, the question may then arise as to why this unity should ever come to be expressed in the diversity that is commonly called speech. In Bhartṛhari's view, it is because the *sphoṭa* itself contains an inner energy *(kratu)* that seeks to burst forth into expression. What appears to be unitary is thus seen to contain all the potentialities of multiplicity and complexity like the seed and the sprout or the egg and the chicken.[18] In the *Vākyapadīya*, Bhartṛhari suggests two ways in which the energy of speech causes the phenomenalization of the *sphoṭa*. On the one hand, there is the pent-up potentiality for bursting forth residing in the *sphoṭa* itself, while on the other hand there is the desire of the speaker to communicate.[19] Unlike thinkers who conceive of language in conventional or utilitarian terms, Bhartṛhari finds language to contain and reveal its own telos. Bhartṛhari, in fact, takes his position to the logical extreme and concludes, in line with the Vedic seers, that from speech *(vāk)* the creation of the whole world proceeds.

It is clear, then, that Bhartṛhari conceives of all beings as born with *śabda*, or speech, already present within. As the child grows, this inner *sphoṭa*, which potentially can be developed into any language, is transformed into the language of the particular speech-community into which the child was born. When the young child utters his first single word ejaculations, "mamma," "dog," "cookie," and so forth, it is clear that whole ideas (as yet incompletely expressed) are being verbalized: for example; "I want mamma!," "See the dog," "Give me a cookie!" Even when a word is used merely in the form of a substantive noun (e.g., "tree"), the verb "to be" is always understood so that what is indicated is really a complete thought (e.g., "It is a tree").[20]

Bhartṛhari observes that man does not speak in individual words. For him the chief reality in linguistic communication is the idea or meaning-whole of the indivisible sentence. Although he sometimes speaks about letters *(varṇa)* or individual words *(pada)* as meaning-bearing units *(sphoṭa)*, it is clear that for Bhartṛhari the true form of the *sphoṭa* is the sentence.[21] Along with this emphasis comes the notion that as we listen to a group of words composing a sentence, there is at some point a flash of insight or intuition (the cartoon "light-going-on" situation) in which the whole meaning of the sentence is comprehended. Bhartṛhari technically terms this experience *pratibhā*.[22] *Pratibhā* in Indian thought is described as a supernormal perception that transcends the ordinary categories of time, space, and causality, and has the capacity to directly "grasp" the real nature of things. The sentence is really a psychic entity, a mental symbol that in itself is the meaning. The mental perception of this meaning-whole *(sphoṭa)* is a case of *pratibhā*. Because the whole sentence meaning is inherently present in the mind of each person, it is quite possible for the *pratibhā* of the *sphoṭa* to be grasped by the listener even before the whole sentence has been uttered. More often, however, inference and reasoning may have to be applied to the words of the sentence so that the individual's cognition is brought to the level where the intuitive grasping *(pratibhā)* of the meaning-whole *(vākya-sphoṭa)* becomes possible.

III *How the* Sphoṭa *Reveals Meaning*

The grammarian *sphoṭa* theory as officially expounded by Bhartṛhari in the *Vākyapadīya* attracted both opponents and supporters. The chief opposition came, at a later time, from the Mīmāṁsaka Kumārila Bhaṭṭa. Kumārila's attack focused on the way in which the *sphoṭa* theory conceived of word-sounds as revealing their meanings. The side of Bhartṛhari in this debate against Kumārila was taken by the skillful philosopher Maṇḍana Miśra. Maṇḍana's work entitled *Sphoṭasiddhi*, which is based on the *Vākyapadīya*, records the confrontation that takes place on this issue of how the word conveys meaning.

In the above definition of *sphoṭa* we have seen how Bhartṛhari maintains that the external word-sound should not be taken as the objective reality since it serves only to reveal the inner word-meaning, which is both a unified whole and the true object. Illustrations have been offered to support Bhartṛhari's view that it is the whole idea that occasions sound and not vice versa. While illustrations from ordinary experience can indicate that the *sphoṭa* theory is not implausible, they can hardly be taken as proof of the theory's logical possibility. The latter requires that the existence of the inner word, as distinct from its sounds, be demonstrated in terms of logical necessity and consistency. This is precisely the task undertaken by Maṇḍana Miśra in his *Sphoṭasiddhi.*[23]

Maṇḍana applies his logical analysis not only to the *sphoṭa* theory but also to the alternative hypothesis put forth by Kumārila. History indicates that Kumārila was the most formidable critic of the *sphoṭa* theory — later writers have offered no new criticism but only repeat Kumārila's arguments. Kumārila, arguing against Bhartṛhari, maintains that the word or *śabda*, whether it be the sentence or the individual word, is nothing more than a collection of word-sounds or spoken letters, and it is with this collection alone that the word-meaning is associated. When such a collection is brought to the mind of the hearer by the sounds uttered by the speaker, the hearer understands the meaning from the sounds alone. No mystical entity, such as *sphoṭa,* need be postulated at all.[24] According to Bhartṛhari, however, "the essence of the *Sphoṭa* doctrine is the idea that the word, mainly in the form of the sentence and secondarily in the form of the individual word and the phoneme [the articulated letter sound], is an entity over and above the sounds and not a mere collection of them and that it is this entity which is the bearer of the meaning."[25] This is the argument in its most general form. Since this argument goes on at great length, in true scholastic form, the chief points are briefly summarized as follows.

Kumārila, the Mīmāṁsaka, opens by identifying *śabda* with the phoneme, or letter sound as uttered. In response, Maṇḍana, arguing from the *Vākyapadīya,* counters by saying that *śabda* refers to the *sphoṭa,* or indivisible word-whole, which is a felt fact in common experience. Kumārila rebuts by saying that it is the grouping together of the phonemes into words *(pada)* that causes the understanding of meaning. To that Maṇḍana replies that because of their ubiquitous and eternal nature, phonemes (as defined by Mīmāṁsakas) can only exist singly and cannot possibly coexist as whole words so as to convey meaning. The inability of the individual phonemes to convey meaning points to the *sphoṭa* as the revealer of meaning.

Kumārila then puts forth three suggestions as to how the phonemes could be grouped together so as to convey meaning, but Maṇḍana finds some difficulty vitiating each suggestion. The first suggestion is that just as a seed will produce a new effect (sprout) when helped by other factors such as soil, sun, and rain, so also the phonemes when combined with a group of helping factors such as being uttered by the same person in a particular sequence will result in the conveying of meaning. To this suggestion Maṇḍana asks, how can being uttered by the same person in a particular sequence make the discrete phonemes c-o-w into a word when each letter-sound vanishes completely before the subsequent one is uttered? In attempting an answer, Kumārila offers his second suggestion, namely, that phonemes leave memory traces *(saṁskāras)* so that the traces of the earlier phonemes together with the utterance of the final phoneme conveys the meaning. But, replies Maṇḍana, *saṁskāras*, or memory traces, like their original phonemes, have only discrete existences vanishing completely before subsequent ones come into existence. When the "w" is uttered, or remembered, the *saṁskāras* for the "c" and "o" will have ceased to exist. There can only be the cognition of one phoneme at a time, and this principle applies equally to the *saṁskāra* and to the original utterance or hearing of the phoneme. Thus, the possibility of phonemes producing *saṁskāras*, or memory traces, gets one no closer to accounting for the generation of a meaning-whole.

Kumārila then takes a new and seemingly potent line of attack. He offers a third suggestion based on an analogy to religious sacrificial practice with its special effect called *apūrva*, or residual force, which is said to lead to heaven. The distinguishing feature of the *saṁskāra* that causes remembrance is that it causes something similar to that which produced it. This, however, is not the case of *apūrva* in a sacrifice. In a sacrifice, the individual acts performed perish immediately, but the *apūrva*, or aftereffect, of the whole sacrifice inheres in the self of the sacrificer as a special kind of potency until it brings the reward of heaven. Its result is thus very different from its cause, and this unusual kind of causal relationship is necessitated by scripture's declaration that the performance of a sacrifice produces such a result. In Kumārila's view, the *apūrva*, or aftereffect, kind of *saṁskāra* that is left by the different letters upon the subject is analogous to such religious leaven. Just as in a sacrifice it is the determinate order of performance by a single agent that is responsible for the spiritual leaven, here also the determinate order of the phonemes uttered by a single person is responsible for the unusual result. So it is when the last phoneme is spoken or heard in the midst of the "leavening" effect of the *saṁskāras* of the previous phonemes that the meaning is conveyed. Maṇḍana answers this argument by pointing out that the analogy is weak. To argue from the *apūrva* of religious merit, which is based on an inference from scripture so as to validate moral law, to the *saṁskāras* of the phonemes rendering language capable of conveying meaning is unjustified. Rather, it is the case that the ordinary memory traces of the phonemes reveal the already existing inherent *sphoṭa,* which provides awareness of the whole and determines the order of the phonemes.

Kumārila's final rebuttal is that in the Mīmāṁsa theory only one new thing (i.e., the special *apūrva*-like power) need be postulated, whereas Maṇḍana postulates two or three new things — a special *saṁskāra* and a *sphoṭa* (and a special power of that *sphoṭa* enabling it to convey meaning). Maṇḍana's reply is that this is not at all what the *Vākyapadīya* maintains. In Bhartṛhari's view the only new thing postulated is the *sphoṭa* itself, and even that need not be postulated since it is directly perceptible. The *saṁskāra* referred to is the common memory trace, which has the same object as that of the uttered phoneme (i.e., the *sphoṭa).* The unified *sphoṭa* was the original cause of the phoneme, and is the end-object of both it and its *saṁskāra.* Thus, no special or illogical power, such as *apūrva,* is postulated. In this logical argument, it seems clear that Kumārila's attempt to identify *śabda* with the uttered phoneme is effectively discredited by the reasoning of Maṇḍana, who has at the same time vindicated the *sphoṭa* theory of Bhartṛhari's *Vākyapadīya.*

Having supported Bhartṛhari's theory on logical grounds, Maṇḍana now gives a detailed analysis of the process by which the *sphoṭa* is cognized. If this analysis is to support the above-mentioned logical argument it must show: (1) how the *sphoṭa* may be comprehended using only the ordinary memory traces of the phonemes, and (2) that the *sphoṭa* is a perceivable entity and not a mere postulation. The process by which the *sphoṭa* is cognized is stated by Maṇḍana in his commentary on *sūtra* 18 of the *Sphoṭasiddhi* as follows. Each spoken sound or letter potentially reveals the whole of the *sphoṭa,* which is already latent in the listener's mind. However, the first letter of the word only dimly begins to evoke that whole meaning in our awareness. The subsequent letters are needed to produce a clear cognition of the whole word. Upon the hearing of the last letter (e.g., "w") along with the memory traces of the previous letters (e.g., "c" and "o"), the complete word (e.g., "cow") stands revealed in a unitary intuition, or *pratibhā.*

The analogy is offered of a jeweler who examines the genuineness of a precious stone. His continuous gaze is really a series of cognitions, each of which perceives the genuineness of the stone but with increasing clarity. Each cognition leaves its *saṁskāra,* or common memory trace. The last cognition, helped by the *saṁskāra* of the previous ones, fully perceives the genuineness of the stone. But for the *saṁskāras* of the intervening cognitions, there would be no difference between the last one and the first one. An important point is that the jeweler is described as "expert," meaning that before beginning the examination he already had the image of a precious stone ingrained in his subconscious, and it was this image (like the inhering *sphoṭa*) that was revealed to the jeweler's mind by his series of partial perceptions.

Another example describes how from a distance one (if one is in India) may mistake a tree for an elephant. But if one keeps on looking at it, the tree is ultimately recognized in its true form. In this situation the truth has been arrived at through a series of errors. The sense organ (in this case the eye) has been in contact with the tree throughout. The errors of perception have had the tree as their object, but the cognitions produced by the eye have had an elephant as their form. When, however, the final or true cognition takes place, it has the form of the tree itself and is one with its object. But this true cognition has been arrived at by going through the series of erroneous peceptions that preceded it. Now this change from error to true perception cannot be explained by factors such as change in distance, since simply standing in the same spot and gazing with intense concentration often produces the described result. "It is the previous cognitions (having tree as the object and the form of the elephant) leaving progressively clearer residual impressions, which become the cause of the clear perception of the tree."[26] There could have been no erroneous cognition of elephant had the tree not been there as an object for the sense organ to come into contact with in the first place. The error, therefore, may be described as misapprehension or vague perception.

In the context of our discussion about words, the *sphoṭa* is similarly said to be the object of the cognitions of each of the phonemes, and yet it at first appears in the form of the phoneme. But through the additional cognitions of the subsequent phonemes, the *sphoṭa* is seen with increasing clarity until with the uttering of the final phoneme the form of the phonemes has become identical with that of the *sphoṭa.*

The paradox as to how the indivisible *sphoṭa* appears as the phonemes, and the phonemes as the parts of the partless *sphoṭa,* is explained as follows. It is the sounds that resemble one another that are the cause of both the error and the final correct cognition of the *sphoṭa.* If, says Bhartṛhari, for the manifestation of two different word-*sphoṭas* one has to make similar movements of the vocal organs, the phonemes produced by these movements appear to be parts of both of the indivisible words.[27] This is an error that is fostered by the construction of such artificial devices as alphabet letters or word syllables, usually for teaching purposes. It is precisely because of this kind of confusion that sentences, words, and phonemes appear to have parts whereas in reality they have none. The obverse of this applies to the *sphoṭa.* From the phenomenal viewpoint the *sphoṭa* "cow," for example, may appear to possess qualities such as accent, speed, loudness, time, place, and person in its utterance. That these are qualities of the phenomenal sounds and not the noumenal *sphoṭa* is what makes possible the common recognition of the word "cow" in spite of its diversity of utterance. From Bhartṛhari's viewpoint, it is this noumenal grounding or basis that makes possible such things as the translation of thought from one phenomenal language to another.

IV *Levels of Language in the* Vākyapadīya

In the foregoing discussion it is clear that, from the *sphoṭa* viewpoint, language may be seen to operate on at least two levels. On one level there is *pratibhā,* or the intuitive flashlike understanding of the sentence-meaning as a whole. On the other level there are the uttered words of the sentence. Bhartṛhari calls the latter *vaikharī vāk* (overt or elaborated speech), while the former is aptly designated as *paśyantī vāk* (speech that through *pratibhā* sees or perceives reality).[28] Between these two levels, says Bhartṛhari, there is a middle, or *madhyamā, vāk* corresponding to the *vākya sphoṭa* in its mental separation into sentence-meaning and a sequence of manifesting word-sounds, none of which have yet been uttered. According to

Bhartṛhari, these are the three levels of language through which *śabda* or *vāk* passes whenever one speaks. *Śabda*, which is at first quite internal, is gradually externalized for the purpose of communication. In this way Bhartṛhari accounts for all cognition as being necessarily identified with language, since these levels of language span the complete continuum of cognition. This is clearly expressed in one of Bhartṛhari's basic tenets: "There is no cognition in the world in which the word does not figure. All knowledge is, as it were, intertwined with the word."[29]

For Bhartṛhari there is no cognition possible without the operation of *śabda*.[30] His conception of the levels of language seems quite logical once this presupposition is accepted. Thought at the *buddhi* or differentiated stage of word-sequences is perhaps best understood as internal speaking. And *pratibhā* or intuition may be seen as a kind of muted speaking. The point being emphasized is that for Bhartṛhari speaking is the essence of consciousness, and the means to all knowledge. And it must also be clearly understood that by "speaking," "language," or "thought" what is meant is *the conveyanace of meaning* — "thinking" here does not primarily refer to concept formation, the drawing of inferences, et cetera; all of which would exist at the two lowest levels *(vaikharī* and *madhyamā*) only. But when "meaning" is identified as intertwined with consciousness (as Bhartṛhari identifies it), this satisfies instances of *pratibhā* as well as instances of more commonplace cognition, and therefore can be held to be logically possible at all levels of *vāk*, including even the very highest (i.e., the *praṇava*).

Behind the discussion of the levels of language in the *Vākyapadīya* is Bhartṛhari's notion of the dynamic limiting function of time *(kālaśakti)*. After setting forth the absolute nature of Brahman as being the one eternal essence of word and consciousness in the first two verses of the *Vākyapadīya*, Bhartṛhari then introduces the notion of time as the power or means by which this one unchanging absolute *(Śabdatattva-Brahman)* manifests itself as the dynamic diversity mankind experiences as creation. Time is the creative power of Brahman, and thus is responsible for the birth, death, and continuity of everything in the cosmos. Time is one, but when broken or limited into sequences appears as moments or actions.[31] These segments of time are mentally categorized as seconds or minutes. Such limited segments of time are then mentally unified into day, week, month, and year. In the same fashion notions of past, present, and future are developed. When time is thought of as an action not yet completed, the notion of the present is established. An action that has been completed is time as past; and an action yet to be completed is time as future. All of ordinary life is sequenced by these three powers of time. Yet, all the while, declares Bhartṛhari, there is really no sequence at all. From the ultimate viewpoint all three powers of time are constantly present. Time is One. Although the effects of the three powers of time (i.e., past, present, and future) are mutually contradictory, they function without causing any disorder in the cosmos. As K. A. S. Iyer puts it, these three powers of time "are like three paths on which objects move about without any confusion. The traffic is regulated. What was at first the path called Future, enters the path called Present and disappears into the path called Past."[32] All of this conjures up in one's mind a few lines from T. S. Eliot: "Time present and time past are both perhaps present in time future, and time future contained in time past."[33] Time in its transformations of past and future is really only One, *Śabdatattva*, the eternal present.

Bhartṛhari enters into this deep discussion of time in relation to the absolute, not as a fascinating metaphysical aside, but to explain how the unitary Word *(Śabdabrahman)* manifests itself in experience as the diversity of words called language. As a grammarian, he is also providing a metaphysical basis for the experience of the tenses past, present, and future in language. And, as will be shortly apparent, it is past and future that have the veiling function of keeping one apart from the absolute eternal present. In religious terms union with the eternal present is union with the Divine, and, for Bhartṛhari, this is the inherent goal toward which all language, all grammar, is reaching.[34]

For the *Vākyapadīya* the nature of the absolute eternal present is word *(śabda)* and consciousness *(caitanya)* inseparably mixed together, self-evident, and revealing of all knowledge. This is *Śabdabrahman*. It is mainly due to the limiting function of time that *Śabdabrahman*, without suffering any loss, assumes differentiation as the intuited *sphoṭa* with its uttered words and manifested meaning. At the lower levels of language, *vaikharī* (overt speech) and *madhyamā* (mental speech), the revealing power of the *sphoṭa* may be likened to a person looking at a landscape through a tube. The tube limits one's vision of the whole landscape, just as the forms of manifested language limit one's mental vision of *Śabdabrahman*. However, the limited vision one does achieve by clear and concentrated looking is real — but it is not the whole of the real. At the lower levels of language, with the limiting forms of spoken words and mental thoughts, repeated "looks" have to be taken at different "views" in an attempt to see the whole. At the upper, or *paśyantī*, level of language it is as if the tube has been taken away from the eye. The limiting forms of manifested speech (like the tube) have been transcended and the final omniscient vision is achieved. In terms of time the final *paśyantī* vision would be the eternal present in its wholeness. At the lower levels, the present would be the portion currently being "looked at" through the limiting forms, the past would be "views" previously seen, and the future, "views" yet to be seen. It is in this sense that Bhartṛhari conceives of the limiting function of time within language.

When one is speaking, therefore, it is through the limiting power of time that the *paśyantī* level of word-consciousness assumes the lower and progressively more differentiated levels of *madhyamā* and *vaikharī*. From the hearer's point of view the process is reversed. The word-sounds *(vaikharī)* and the inner word-meanings *(madhyamā)* are both initially cognized under the sequence of time until, with the final perception of the whole *(vākya-sphoṭa)*, the level of *paśyanti* is manifested. In this state of inner intuition noumenal knowledge dawns, and all differentiation due to the sequence of time is transcended.

Having seen how the levels of language fit into the overall metaphysics of the *Vākyapadīya*, each level will now be examined in somewhat more detail. *Vaikharī* is the most external and differentiated level in which *vāk* is commonly uttered by the speaker and heard by the hearer. It is *prāṇa*, or breath, that enables the organs of articulation and hearing to produce and perceive sounds in a temporal sequence. *Prāṇa* may therefore be taken as the instrumental cause of *vaikharī vāk*. The chief characteristic of *vaikharī vāk* is that it has a fully developed temporal sequence. At this level individual peculiarities of the speaker (e.g., accent) are present along with the linguistically relevant parts of speech.

Going further inward, as it were, *madhyamā vāk* is the next level and its association is chiefly with the mind or intellect *(buddhi)*. It is the idea or series of words as conceived by the mind after hearing or before speaking out. It may be thought of as inward speech. All the parts of speech that are linguistically relevant to the sentence are present here in a latent form. At this level a variety of manifestation is possible. The same *sphoṭa* or meaning is capable of being revealed by a variety of forms of *madhyamā*, depending on the language adopted. Although there is not full temporal sequence of the kind experienced in spoken words, word and meaning are still distinct and word order is present. Therefore, temporal sequence must also be present along with its instrumental cause, *prāṇa*.

The next and innermost stage is *paśyantī vāk*. *Paśyantī* is the direct experience of the *vākya-sphoṭa* — of meaning as a noumenal whole. At this level there is no distinction between the word and the meaning and there is no temporal sequence. All such phenomenal differentiations drop away with the intuition of the pure meaning in itself. Yet there is present at this level a kind of "going-out" or desire for expression. This is the "instinct" or telos inherent in the *paśyanti* vision that may be said to motivate the phenomenalization into sentences and words so that communication occurs. Thus the Vedic vision of the *ṛṣi*, which in itself is *paśyantī*, becomes phenomenalized so that by its uttered word men might rise above their ignorance and be grasped in their cognition by the revelation of ultimate reality. Therefore, there is a sense in which Veda is identified as *paśyantī vāk*. Since *paśyantī* is, by definition, beyond the level of differentiated cognition, it is impossible to define it in word-sentences. It is at the level of direct intuition and therefore must be finally understood through experience.

Nevertheless, there has been no dearth of speculation over the exact nature of *paśyantī* and the possibility of yet a higher level of language, that is, *parā vāk*. It is quite possible that Bhartṛhari himself may have conceived of a fourth, or *parā vāk*, level. The commentary on I:142 does quote, among numerous other passages, *Ṛg Veda* I:164:45, which refers to four levels of *vāk*. Of these four, three remain hidden in the cave or the inner self; only the fourth is spoken by man as his external language. In this regard, K. A. S. Iyer offers an interesting observation on the *Vākyapadīya* itself. He points out that a very obvious parallel seems to exist between its structure and contents, and the levels of *vāk*. The first chapter concentrates a great deal on Brahman, the undifferentiated ultimate reality, to which the *paśyantī vāk* is very near. In the second chapter the *vākya-sphoṭa* is the subject with its paradox of containing both the differentiation of the sentence-words and the unitary meaning at the same time. This parallels the *madhyamā* level of *vāk*. The third chapter concentrates almost totally on analysis of parts of speech and their differentiation, which clearly seems identical with the realm of *vaikharī vāk*. Iyer finds support for such a parallelism from Helārāja. If this interpretation is assumed, then the parallel to the level of *parā vāk* might well be taken as the whole of the *Vākyapadīya;* for in this work it is the indivisible whole of the speaking act, or better yet, "speech itself," that Bhartṛhari is analyzing. As Iyer observes, it is remarkable how Bhartṛhari, throughout the *Vākyapadīya,* is ever conscious of the highest word-principle, the *Śabdatattva* — "Brahman out of which the whole cosmos and our experience of it consisting of an infinite variety of cognitions, objects and words expressive of them, are manifested."[35]

Although the whole of Bhartṛhari's *Vākyapadīya* has exerted a strong influence upon subsequent Indian thought, the notion of levels of language and especially of *parā vāk* has formed the foundation for the Kashmir Pratýabhijñā school and its famous exponents Utpala and Abhinavagupta. The Kashmir school fully adopts the *Vākyapadīya* conception of *parā vāk* as an intertwining of word and consciousness. These Kashmir philosophers illustrate what is meant by using the following analogy. A crystal has something in common with consciousness, namely, that it can reflect an object. But the significant difference between a crystal and *parā vāk* is that when a crystal reflects an object, it is conscious neither that it is reflecting an object, nor of what the object is that is being reflected. But when one knows something, one is aware that it is oneself that is doing the knowing, and also what the object is that is known.[36] This ability for self-conscious reflection and knowing is, according to the *Vākyapadīya,* potentially present in all human beings at birth, and is even shared by the animals as their basic instincts.[37]

A modern scholar, Gaurinath Sastri, has made a careful comparative study between the classification of *vāk* as found in the *Vākyapadīya* and in the Kashmir Śaiva writers.[38] He concludes that although the two systems do not differ significantly, various distinctions can be made. Sastri points out that for Bhartṛhari the supreme reality is conceived of in terms of *śabda* or *vāk* in such a way that there is no real difference between *Śabdabrahman* and *Parabrahman* — they merely represent two aspects of the same supreme *Śabda.* Consequently, *Śabda Brahman* is synomous with *Paśyantī* and *Para Brahman* with *Parā Vāk.* According to Kashmir thought, however, *parā vāk* is given a subtle logical distinction in that it is described as a power of the supreme reality *Parama Śiva* — yet both *Parama Śiva* and his power *parā vāk* are held to be identical in essence. Whereas for Bhartṛhari and his followers *parā vāk* is taken to be independent and self-subsistent, the Kashmir writers place *parā vāk* in a dependent relationship to *Parama Śiva. Parama Śiva* is described as the substantive or the powerful, while *parā vāk* is the attribute or the power. Sastri concludes his comparison by suggesting that Bhartṛhari's writing was earlier than that of the Kashmir writers, and that their subsequent speculations have led to a different conception of *parā vāk* — but a difference that is more logical than real in its nature. However, it may also be that the distinction insisted on by the Kashmir philosophers is a direct result of Bhartṛhari's equation of *Paśyantī* (from the root *dṛs* — to see in the present time) with the supreme reality. "Seeing" admits a multiplicity in that relation with an object is implied, and this is clearly unacceptable as a description of the ultimate necessitating a higher level of *vāk*.[39]

Yet another post-*Vākyapadīya* school, South India Śaivism (under the Pallava Kings of the seventh century), also utilized the notion of *parā vāk*. But the Śaiva Siddhānta, as this school came to be known, strongly disagrees with the *Vākyapadīya*. From the Śaiva Siddhānta viewpoint Bhartṛhari's interpretation is criticized in a fashion similar to the previously mentioned objection of Jayantabhaṭṭa. In the Śaiva Siddhānta view *śabda* is not self-revealing, but serves only to illuminate the meaning that is located in the independently existing object *(artha)*. Because of this basic disagreement in presupposition, the interpretation given to the four levels of *vāk*, and especially to that of *parā vāk*, is quite different from that offered by Bhartṛhari.[40]

The levels of language analyzed by Bhartṛhari in the *Vākyapadīya* are more than just linguistic theory or theological speculation. They are intimately connected with the goal or purpose for living and the practical discipline for its realization. In the *vṛtti* on *Vākyapadīya* 1:131 Bhartṛhari identifies two distinct goals that may be realized through the careful study and use of language. The knowledge and correct use of words enables one to achieve happiness or spiritual merit in this life and in heaven. In another place the commentary (on *Vākyapadīya* I:14) clearly states that the use of corrupt forms of language is a cause of sin, and that the correct use of language not only reveals knowledge but also results in the acquiring of spiritual merit. That is the first goal or "flower" *(puspita)* the study of grammar can bring. The second goal, significantly called the "fruit" *(phalita)*, includes the first but goes well beyond — it is the realization of *mokṣa*, or complete union with *Śabdabrahman*. In reaching *mokṣa* the knowledge and correct use of words is but the first step on the path.[41] What are the subsequent steps? Here the *Vākyapadīya* becomes vague, although some clues are offered.

In discussing the different ways that various schools of his day describe the realization of Brahman, Bhartṛhari begins with a view which seems to be his own: "The attainment of Brahman is nothing more than going beyond the knot *[granthi]* of the ego-sense in the form of 'I' and 'Mine.' "[42] Later on in the commentary on *kārikā* I:130 Bhartṛhari suggests how this "knot" of ego-sense can be overcome: "The Great Word-Bull is the Lord of all, endowed with all powers. Those who know the process of union with the Word *[vāgyoga]* break the knot of ego-sense and are merged into it, with complete absence of differentation."[43] Here the word *vāgyoga* clearly points to some kind of Yoga or meditation that arrests the ordinary mental processes. In ordinary consciousness one habitually limits one's perceptions of reality to cognizable "bits" (e.g., the series of "views" through the tube) so that time sequence and the differentation of the One into the many appears. A further hint as to the exact nature of this Yoga occurs in *kārikā* I:20, which says "that words appear like reflections in the *Brahman* in the case of those who practise the *Yoga* of the Word *(śabdapūrvayoga)*."[44] Throughout the *Vākyapadīya* wherever these two terms *vāgyoga* and *śabdapūrvayoga* occur, the Yoga for transcending word sequence is clearly in the context of the ascending levels of language — *vaikharī*, *madhyamā*, *paśyantī*. As was noted above, both spoken language *(vaikharī)* and inner thought *(madhyamā)* are characterized as being "limited views" and therefore necessarily in time sequence. Only when one reaches the ultimate level of *paśyantī*, where, as it were, one has shed the limiting "tubes" of conceptual speech and thought, is the pure mental vision *(pratibhā)* of the whole Divine Word known. But this kind of knowing is different from the knowing of one's ordinary consciousness where "I" the subject describe some separate object — as is done in science, logic, and all scholastic disciplines. While the correct knowledge of grammar and use of words is important and productive of spiritual merit *(dharma)*, it will not enable one to reach *mokṣa*, or union with the Divine Word. For that, the special Yoga that Bhartṛhari calls *śabdapūrvayoga* or *vāgyoga* is required.

Unfortunately, the *Vākyapadīya* seems to assume the reader's familiarity with the practice of *śabdapūrvayoga*. The closest thing to a detailed description occurs in the commentary on *kārikā* I:123. The elimination of all differentation or sequence seems to be the chief characteristic of these verses, which K. A. S. Iyer translates as follows:

Taking his stand on the essence of the Word lying beyond the activity of breath *(prāṇa)*, resting in one's self with all sequence eliminated,
After having purified speech and after having rested it on the mind, after having broken its bonds and made it bond-free, After having reached the inner Light, he with his knots cut, becomes united with the Supreme Light.[45]

Although Bhartṛhari is emphatic that the study of the correct use and meaning of *vāk* is a means of attaining *mokṣa*, he goes no further in describing the Yoga required or the different stages of that spiritual ascent. As Iyer points out, Bhartṛhari seems to do little more than to observe the levels of *vāk*, particularly the *vaikharī*, *madhyamā*, and *paśyantī*, and indirectly suggest that they are somehow connected with the process of ascent of *mokṣa*.[46] In the following chapter an attempt will be made at suggesting the detailed discipline of *śabdapūrvayoga* that Bhartṛhari seems to have assumed throughout the *Vākyapadīya*.

CHAPTER 3

The Yoga Psychology Underlying Bhartrhari's Vakyapadiya

I *Yoga: A Basic Assumption in Indian Thought*

YOGA was the traditional psychology of India in Bhartṛhari's day, and indeed has continued to occupy that status in the minds of most Indians right up to the present. It is only during the last few decades that the psychology taught in Indian universities and colleges has come to be modern empirical or scientific psychology. Today, although modern Western psychology may be taught in the universities, the basic psychology assumed and accepted by most Indians is still the same Yoga psychology that reached the peak of its development during the Gupta period. The classic formulation of traditional Yoga psychology is the *Yoga Sūtras* of Patañjali, which are usually dated around A.D. 300. The important commentary or *bhāṣya* on the *Yoga Sūtras* is attributed to Vyāsa, and seems to be contemporary with Bhartṛhari. Later, an explanation, or *ṭīkā*, called the *Tattva-Vāicāradī*, written by Vācaspati Miśra, was added. The *Yoga Sūtras* with the *Commentary* and *Explanation* have been translated into English by both James H. Woods and Rāma Prasāda.[1]

Although the *Yoga Sūtras* are written within the context of the Sāṅkhya school of metaphysics, the focus throughout is on the analysis of the psychological processes commonly accepted by all of the various schools — orthodox and heterodox alike. Within Indian thought it seems clear that just as certain conceptions such as *karma* (the moral law) and *saṁsāra* (rebirth) are taken as basic to all Hindu and Buddhist schools, so also there are certain psychological conceptions such as cognitive traces *(saṁskāras)* that are seen to exist in and through the specific differences of the various schools as a kind of commonly understood psychology. Jadunath Sinha supports this contention in his finding that the Indian psychological conception of supersensuous mental perception or intuition *(pratibhā)* is found in all schools with the exception of the Cārvāka and the Mīmāṁsā.[2] T. H. Stcherbatsky, the eminent Russian scholar of Buddhism, observes that Yogic trance *(samādhi)* and Yogic courses for the training of the mind in the achievement of *mokṣa* or *nirvāṇa (yoga-marga)* appear in virtually all Indian schools of thought — be they Hindu, Buddhist, or Jaina.[3] And Mircea Eliade, in his well-known book *Yoga: Immortality and Freedom*, maintains that Yoga is one of the four basic motifs of all Indian thought.[4]

An understanding of this commonly assumed Yoga psychology is necessary if Bhartṛhari's *Vākyapadīya* (and his thought generally) is to be seen in its full perspective. A complete analysis of the *Vākyapadīya* must include both its philosophical aspect (i.e., the metaphysical inquiry into the nature of meaning in language), and its psychological aspect (i.e., the Yoga explanation of the processes required for communicating meaning at the lower level of language, and the discipline for becoming one with the Divine Word, *śabdapūrvayoga*). In current writing on the *Vākyapadīya* scholars such as K. A. S. Iyer and G. Sastri have concentrated on the first aspect, the metaphysics, and largely neglected the second, the psychological and practical aspects.[5] In this study a conscious effort is made to give equal treatment to both aspects. In the previous chapter, the metaphysics of the *Vākyapadīya* was the point of focus. In this chapter an attempt is made at describing the Yoga psychology assumed by Bhartṛhari, but often left unstated. Not only will this provide a more complete picture of Bhartṛhari's theory of language; it will also suggest in detail what he may have meant by *śabdapūrvayoga* as a discipline for meditation upon the Divine Word until *mokṣa*, or union with *Śabdabrahman*, is realized.

II *The Structure of Consciousness as Śabdabrahman*

The *Vākyapadīya* describes consciousness as an intertwined unity of cognition and word that constantly seeks to manifest itself in speech. A conception of consciousness that seems parallel to Bhartṛhari's description is found in the *Yoga Sūtra* analysis of Īśvara's omniscience.[6] Here the intertwining of word and meaning in consciousness is seen in its purest form. Within Īśvara's consciousness is the seed form of all words, which remains constant throughout the various manifestations and dissolutions of each cycle of creation. Every new cycle arises out of the need of Īśvara's consciousness to burst forth into expression. Thus Īśvara, or the Lord, is described as having two characteristics: (1) a pure consciousness of perfect quality *(sattva)*, and (2) as being the germ or seed *(bīja)* of omniscience at its utmost excellence.[7]

The detailed description of this special consciousness of Īśvara is undertaken in Yoga psychology through an analysis of one's own experience of consciousness. In one's ordinary experience of consciousness three aspects or substantive qualities *(guṇas)* are found: *sattva,* which is brightness or intelligence; *rajas,* which is passion or energy; and *tamas,* which is dullness or inertia. Although each of these *guṇas* keeps its own separate identity, no individual *guṇa* ever exists independently. Rather, the three *guṇas* are always necessarily found together like three strands of a rope. However, the proportionate composition of consciousness assigned to each of the *guṇas* is constantly changing.[8] Only the predominant *guṇa* will be easily recognized in a particular thought. The other two *guṇas* will be present but subordinate, and therefore their presence will have to be determined by inference.

In the case of Īśvara, his consciousness is described as being completely dominated by pure *sattva* (although some *rajas* and *tamas* must also be present). Within this *sattva* there is a teleology that ensures the reappearance of Īśvara in each new creation for the purpose of communicating to all beings his omniscient knowledge, so that they may, with the help of his grace, attain *mokṣa.* The psychological mechanism by which Īśvara's reappearance in each new creation is ensured is as follows. At the end of each creation, Īśvara freely wishes that his *sattva* consciousness should appear again at the time of the next creation. This wish leaves behind a *saṁskāra,* or mental potency, which acts as a "seed state" from which Īśvara blossoms afresh in each new creation. The underlying metaphysical assumption here is that Brahman freely phenomenalizes himself as Īśvara (as an act of grace) so as to provide the means (i.e., the revelation of the Veda) by which one can attain *mokṣa.* On the psychological level, this revelation, if it is to be capable of human understanding, must function through human cognition. Thus there is a kind of continuum between Īśvara's *sattva* and that of the lowest being *(jīva).*

The matchless perfection of Īśvara's *sattva* consciousness is evident in, and attested to, by his omniscience, which he communicates to the *ṛṣis* as scriptural truth, or *āgama* (including *śruti, smṛti,* the epics and the Purāṇas). The psychological means by which this communication takes place is technically referred to as *viśiṣṭopahita* (intuition caused by the grace of a special person). The *ṛṣi* supersensuously sees directly into the omniscience incarnated in Īśvara's *sattva* and reveals it to other men in the manifested form of uttered speech — Veda, the authoritative *vāk*. Īśvara is thus named both the first knower and the first teacher, who, out of grace, gives to the great *ṛṣis* a direct vision of that which is the essence of all language and all revelation — namely, his own consciousness. Within each creation, at least, this unity of omniscience and consciousness, which is Īśvara's *sattva*, is timeless in that it continues on unchanging although the limitations necessary for human language are constantly being placed upon it.[9] It is the dynamic ground upon which all language and knowledge rests, and from which all speech evolves. Scriptural truth, both as the revealed word *(śruti)* and the remembered writings of tradition *(smṛti)*, is really the authoritative verbalization of Īśvara's *sattva*, and may therefore be taken as the expression of the true nature of consciousness.[10] All this is expressed in the one mystic symbol, AUM, which, when spoken, connotes Īśvara with all his power for omniscience.

Īśvara, as described above, represents for Yoga psychology the pure ideal upon which the Yogin, or devotee, should focus in his daily practice. He is defined as a special kind of being who is free from or untouched by instinctual drives *(kleśas)* and the actions or thoughts performed as a result of such drives *(karma)*.[11] When all these aspects of psychological functioning are deleted, what is left is Īśvara's omniscient consciousness with its compassionate telos for communication. It is in this sense that Īśvara is a close parallel to the *Vākyapadīya* conception of consciousness as a given unity of thought and meaning. The Yoga conception of Īśvara provides, as required by the *Vākyapadīya*, that consciousness contain within it the seed state of omniscience. And just as the *Yoga Sūtras* take this omniscient consciousness as the universal basis for the scriptural truth *(āgama)* of the *ṛṣis*, so also Bhartṛhari conceives of *āgama* as necessarily existing within all beings and providing the basis for their *pratibhā* experience. Although there may be some differences in Bhartṛhari's concept of *āgama*, the main outline of his conception is in agreement with that of Patañjali.[12] For Bhartṛhari, Brahman is conceived of as the omniscient word-principle — the *Śabdatattva*. Bhartṛhari maintains that the Veda is not only the means of attaining *mokṣa*, but is also the image *(anukāra)* of Brahman. This is almost identical to the *Yoga Sūtra* description of Īśvara as the ever free and eternal Lord whose omniscience, verbalized as Veda, enables beings to achieve *mokṣa*.

While all this indicates good grounds for the use of Patañjali's psychological analysis of Īśvara as a parallel against which to interpret Bhartṛhari's conception of reality as word-consciousness or *Śabdabrahman,* one difference does exist at the level of the highest metaphysical speculation. The Yoga system is ultimately a duality between pure consciousness *(puruṣa)* and nonintelligent matter *(prakṛti).* Consequently, Vācaspati points out that Īśvara's *sattva* does not possess the power of consciousness since *sattva* is nonintelligent in its own nature.[13] From the viewpoint of Sāṅkhya/Yoga metaphysics, *sattva,* as a manifestation of *prakṛti,* only appears to have intelligence as a result of *avidyā* or the beginningless wrong identification between *puruṣa* and *prakṛti.*[14] The nature of *prakṛti* is also exemplified in terms of causation, namely, that the cause persists in all its effects and therefore the nature of the cause can be deduced by observing what persists in the effects. For example, gold may be seen to exist in all objects made from gold. By looking at them it can be inferred that gold is the original material out of which they were all made.

Although *sphoṭa* theory is nondualistic, there is evidence of a similar sort of causal argument. In the *vṛtti* on the *Vākyapadīya* I:123, it is stated that our knowledge of everything in the world is interwoven with the word. Knowledge is by its nature in the form of words. In order to cognize any object, we must first cognize the word relating to it. Therefore, since all manifestations of Brahman are intertwined with the word, so also the root cause of all such manifestations, Brahman, must be of the nature of the word *(Śabdatattva).* From the *sphoṭa* viewpoint, therefore, Īśvara's omniscient *sattva,* as the root cause of all speech, needs no outside illumination (such as *puruṣa*); for as the ultimate Word-Principle *(Śabdatattva)* it is self-luminous. Now, from the Yoga standpoint, for the practical purpose of our psychological experience Īśvara's *sattva* also appears to us as self-illuminated in nature. It is only at the level of *mokṣa,* or final discrimination, leading directly to *kaivalya* (realization of the *puruṣa*'s existence as independent and free from the fetters of *prakṛti*), that the Sāṁkhya/Yoga dualistic metaphysics results in a total break with the *sphoṭa* theory. At the empirical level of verbal communication between individuals, however, there is no difficulty, since for psychological purposes both Yoga and *sphoṭa* treat consciousness as being self-manifesting.[15]

The above discussion shows that in the Yoga conception of Īśvara there is a ready-made basis for a psychological interpretation of the

Vākyapadīya view of consciousness. In that discussion the psychological mechanism by which the noumenal word forms of Īśvara or the *Śabdatattva* exist from one cycle of creation to the next was identified as *saṁskāra. Saṁskāra* is defined as follows. When a particular mental state *(citta vṛtti)* passes away into another, it does not totally disappear but is preserved within consciousness as a latent form or *saṁskāra.*[16] Such *saṁskāras* are always tending to manifest themselves anew, and therefore are also referred to as *bīja*, or seed states. Īśvara's state of *sattvic* omniscience is described as *bīja* in that his matured omniscience lays down the seeds for its own eternal continuance (both within and between creations). The "seed" connotation emphasizes potency, which is the essential characteristic of *saṁskāra.* On the analogy of the seed and the sprout, *saṁskāras* are seen to be self-perpetuating in nature. A particular mental state, or *citta vṛtti,* results in a like *saṁskāra,* which is always attempting to manifest itself in another mental state similar to the first. Thus, there is a self-generating cycle from mental state to *saṁskāras* to mental state, and so on. In Yoga thinking this cycle is beginningless (i.e., it has always been going on), but is not necessarily endless. Although the repetition of the same series of mental state–*saṁskāra*–mental state results in the establishing and strengthening of habit patterns *(vāsanās),* which are likened to "roots" that have grown deep within the "soil" of consciousness, the continual practicing of an opposing *saṁskāra* series will eventually weaken and render the "root," or *vāsanā,* of the less-reinforced series impotent.

In Yoga thought such *saṁskāra* series or *vāsanās* are categorized as either (1) *kliṣṭa* (afflicted by ignorance), obstructing and leading away from the revelation of knowledge or insight *(prajñā);* or (2) *akliṣṭa* (unafflicted), leading toward *prajñā.*[17] Seen in this perspective, *citta,* or consciousness, is like a constantly moving river whose flow can go in either of two directions (or both ways at the same time).[18] Through the *saṁskāra* series resulting from Īśvara's beginningless bestowing of the Veda within consciousness, the mind has an inherent tendency toward knowledge and the revelation of Brahman. But through the *kliṣṭa saṁskāra* series composed of beginningless ignorance *(avidyā)* and egoity *(asmitā)* (which characterize the endless round of birth-death-rebirth, or *saṁsāra*) the mind has an innate tendency toward ignorance.[19] The teleology of consciousness (via the grace of Īśvara), however, ensures that the will to realize knowledge is never lost in man — thus the innate overall tendency of consciousness is to flow in the direction of knowledge.

How does this Yoga analysis of consciousness and its *saṁskāra* function apply to the *Vākyapadīya*? *Sphoṭa* theory defines consciousness as an intertwined unity of cognition and word, which constantly seeks to manifest itself in speech. In the Yoga analysis of consciousness we have seen how the *sattva* aspect of *citta* is beginninglessly endowed with the word forms or meanings of the Veda because of the grace of Īśvara. These *sattvic* word forms are equivalent to Bhartṛhari's *vākya-sphoṭas,* or sentence meanings. *Saṁskāra* series provide the psychological process by which the *sphoṭas* become and continue as *vṛttis,* or states within consciousness. Such a primordial noumenal *sphoṭa* is psychologically analyzed as a concentrated insight *(prajñā)* that exists as an undisturbed succession of pure *akliṣṭa saṁskāra.* It does not fluctuate or change, nor does it require any supporting object *(ālambana)* since it is itself the substrattum — the eternal universal essence upon which all phenomenal language manifestations of that word depend.[20] As *prajñā,* or pure intuition, it is unitary, partless, and free from the predicate relations that characterize ordinary speech. Yet as consciousness, it contains in addition to this pure *sattvic* intuition elements of *tamas* and *rajas* (especially the latter), which provide the material and motive force for the phenomenalization of the *sphoṭa* into thought and speech. Thus, the inherent telos of consciousness is toward the self-revelation and communication of which Bhartṛhari speaks.

The actual processes of phenomenalization have not as yet been analyzed. Up to this point, the focus has been on the analysis of consciousness at the noumenal or *paśyantī* level in order to demonstrate its nature as including cognition, word-meaning, and the desire for speech. The mention of phenomenalization here is simply to indicate that the *rajas* and *tamas* aspects of consciousness provide the potential for its various particular manifestations.

III *Psychological Processes in Speaking*

In the above mentioned examination of the nature of consciousness, a description has been offered of how consciousness could contain within itself (in a potential state) word, cognition, and the desire for expression. This level of consciousness has been shown to be synonymous with *paśyantī vāk* or *Śabdabrahman* in the *Vākyapadīya.* Here the *sphoṭa* exists in an undifferentiated state. It is simply the *vāk* of Īśvara pervasively existing within undifferentiated consciousness in eternally continuous pure *sattva saṁskāra* series. In it there is no distinction between word and meaning, but only the constant presence of meaning as a whole. There is present, however, "a going out," a desire for expression. It is this characteristic of consciousness that will be focused on now.

An introspective examination of one's initial experience in the act of speaking provides the starting point. At its earliest genesis the speaking act would seem to involve the following: some kind of mental effort to control or tune out distracting sensations and thoughts, an inwardly focused concentration of the mind, and an effort of the mind to bring into self-awareness some idea (or glimpse of reality) that is only vaguely within our ken. Although we may feel very sure of its presence just beyond the fringes of our conscious awareness, and although we may find ourselves impelled by a great desire to reveal that idea in discursive thought, a strong effort at concentrated thinking is often required before any clear conception of it is mentally achieved. Even then one may well feel dissatisfied in that the laboriously conceived conceptualization proves to be so inadequate and incomplete in comparison with one's direct intuition of the noumenal "idea" that remains stubbornly transcendent in the face of all one's attempts to capture it in discrete thought. Yet the more persistently and intensely one thinks, the clearer one's corresponding intuition of the object often becomes. But thinking it is not enough. One is also conscious of a compulsion to manifest one's inner thought in speech (or writing), for only then does the urge for the revelation of the hidden idea seem fully satisfied. According to Bhartṛhari, it is this urge or inner energy *(kratu)* that is responsible for the whole process of the individuation of consciousness and the expression of *sphoṭa* in both inner thought and outer speech.[21]

Bhartṛhari maintains that this *kratu*, or inner energy, is a quality of the *sphoṭa* itself. But the telos of *kratu* to burst forth *(sphuṭ)* into disclosure is experienced within self-awareness in two forms. On the one hand, there is the pent-up energy for disclosure residing in the *sphoṭa*, while on the other hand there is the epistemic urge of the subjective consciousness and its desire, as a speaker, to communicate.[22] According to Yoga, what would be the psychological processes involved in speaking forth the *sphoṭa*?

In Yoga theory it is clear that the energy aspect of any manifestation of consciousness will be directly attributable to *rajas*. We have already described consciousness in its unmanifested state *(paśyantī vāk)* as containing the omniscience bestowed by Īśvara's *sattva*. The characteristic of this state is that in it *sattva* predominates over *rajas* and *tamas* in a steady flow of Īśvara's omniscient ideas (Vedas). These ideas or unmanifested *sphoṭas* are but limitations within *sattva* of the pure universal knowledge of consciousness. At this level of collective consciousness *(buddhitattva)*, there is no subject-object distinction, and, as Vyāsa puts it, "all we can say is that it exists."[23] This *buddhitattva* is consciousness in its most universal form, containing within it all the *buddhis*, or intellects, of individuals and potentially all the matter of which the gross world is formed. Thus it is also referred to as *mahat*, or "the great one," in Yoga writings.

Now, as a result of the teleology inherent in consciousness (i.e., the grace of Īśvara), the *buddhitattva* is affected by its own pent-up *rajas* activity, which posits itself as ego *(ahaṁkāra)*. This is the sense of "I-ness," "me," or "mine." Due to the increasing preponderance of *rajas guṇa* in the originally pure *sattva* of *buddhi*, the *buddhi* consciousness transforms itself into the ego, the subject or the knower. But at this first phase of ego manifestation the ego, although conscious of itself, has as yet no other content to know since the *tamas guṇa* is still under suppression. This bare "I-ness" is a preponderance of *rajas* as manifested by *sattva*, which knows itself to be active and holds itself as the permanent energizing activity of all the phenomena of life.[24] Still, however, there is no subject-object distinction and therefore the *sphoṭas* inherent in consciousness can only be known as a general datum of consciousness but with the characteristic of "I-ness" or "mine." *Sphoṭa* at this level is described as the subtle inner word *(sūkṣmā vāk)* that becomes the knower *(jñātā)*, and then in order to reveal himself becomes the external word.[25] In the Yoga description the *ahaṁkāra*, or ego, is equivalent to the *sūkṣmā vāk*, and *rajas* to the *sakti*, or power of *vāk* for self-manifestation.

The next level of manifestation occurs when the *buddhi* consciousness, through the *ahaṁkāra*, turns back upon itself and divides into a part that sees and a part that is seen — the subject-object distinction that characterizes thought. According to Yoga theory, consciousness accomplishes this involutional bifurcation by virtue of the germs of subjectivity and objectivity that the *guṇas* of consciousness contain within themselves. At the initial *ahaṁkāra* level these two sides of subject and object exist, but only in an implicit way within the bare self-awareness. This bifurcated individuation of the *buddhi* through the *ahaṁkāra* occurs by the instrumental activity of *rajas* in evolving, on the one hand a *sattva* preponderance, and on the other a *tamas* preponderance of consciousness.

Following first the *rajas*-produced *sattva* preponderance, it is seen as a continuing individuation of the *buddhitattva*, or collective consciousness — since the latter was already characterized as having a dominance of *sattva*. By the further activity of *rajas*, the *sattva* consciousness through the *ahaṁkāra* develops itself into: the five cognitive senses *(jñanendriya)* of vision, touch, smell, taste, and hearing; the five faculties of action *(karmendriya)* — speaking, handling, locomotion, evacuation, and sexual generation; and the *prāṇas*, or *vayus* (psychomotor activities that help both action and cognition and are the life-force manifestations of *rajas*). Also formed by the *rajas* activity in the *sattva* preponderance is a further specialization of the *ahaṁkāra* as *manas* — the instrument whereby the *ahaṁkāra* directly connects itself with the cognitive and conative senses. It is in this manner that Yoga theory envisages the collective consciousness of the *buddhitattva* being individuated into the intellects (individual *buddhis*) of finite persons. Dasgupta helpfully summarizes this *rajas*-produced individuation of *citta:*

> The individual ahaṁkâras and senses are related to the individual buddhis by his developing sattva determinations from which they had come into being. Each buddhi with its own group of ahaṁkāra (ego) and sense-evolutes thus forms a microcosm separate from similar other buddhis with their associated groups. So far therefore as knowledge is subject to sense-influence and the ego, it is different for each individual, but so far as a general mind *(kāraṇa buddhi)* apart from sense knowledge is concerned, there is a community of all buddhis in the buddhitattva. Even there, however, each buddhi is separated from other buddhis by its own peculiarly associated ignorance *(avidyā)*.[26]

From the viewpoint of the *Vākyapadīya*, the above situation is interpreted as follows. At the collective level each *buddhi* has incorporated in its particular *avidyā vāsanās* accumulated from word usage in previous lives. These are seed forms of the inherent *śabda* vocalization patterns, which, as Bhartṛhari points out, are seen to already exist in the newborn baby who does not yet know any language. This is the expressive element of *sphoṭa* in its potential state. But, insofar as the individual *buddhi* participates in the general mind (the *buddhitattva*), the *sattva* there encountered contains seed forms of the inherent meanings (described above as Vedic *akliṣṭa saṁskāra* series, bestowed by the grace of Īśvara). These seeds are the meaning elements *(artha)* in potential form, and are also referred to as the expressed aspect of the *sphoṭa*.

On the other side of the bifurcation by the activity of *rajas*, the *tamas guṇa* of the *buddhitattva* individuates through the *ahaṁkāra* into the five *tanmātras*, or subtle elements, which, by a further evolution of themselves, produce the five gross elements of matter. The *tamas guṇa* by itself is inert mass, but in combination with *rajas* becomes fully dynamic and vibrant — in somewhat the same sense as matter is conceived as moving electrical energy charges in modern physics and chemistry. In its state as mere mass, *tamas* is referred to as *bhūtādi*. By its combination with differing amounts of energy *(rajas)*, the *bhūtādi* is individuated into various *tanmātras* or aggregations of the original mass-units. Due to their particular collocations of mass and energy, the *tanmātras* possess the potential physical qualities of sound *(śabda)*, touch *(sparśa)*, color or shape *(rūpa)*, flavor or taste *(rasa)*, and smell *(gandha)*. These *tanmatras* are the subtle material counterparts of the five cognitive senses that formed part of the *rajas-sattva* individuation described above.

Consciousness, or *citta*, having reached the furthest limit of its *rajas* individuation by producing the senses and *manas* on the one side and the material atoms on the other, should not be thought of as having reached the end of its process of change. The underlying principle of *citta*'s transformation is concisely stated by Dasgupta: "The order of succession is not from whole to parts nor from parts to whole but ever from a relatively less differentiated, less determinate, less coherent whole to a relatively more determinate, more coherent whole. . . . Increasing differentiation proceeds *pari passu* with increasing integration within the evolving whole."[27] Seen in its cosmic perspective, the *rajas*-energized transformation of *sattva* and *tamas* toward both individuation and integration results in a totality of mass, energy, and illumination that remains constant throughout its diversity of collocations. Although manifestations of the *guṇas* within individual *buddhis* may appear to be subject to growth and decay, the *guṇas* taken in the totality of their manifested and unmanifested *citta* are a cosmic constant (with no overall increase or decrease but having a continuous circular flow within the system as a whole).

In Yoga theory it seems clear that *rajas* activity provides the psychological basis required for the "instinctive urge" to phenomenalize the *sphoṭa*. *Rajas* in its pent-up state within the *buddhitattva* is a clear description of the energy for disclosure *(sphuṭ)* that Bhartṛhari conceives of as residing within the *sphoṭa*. And in its individuation of the *buddhitattva* through the *ahaṁkāra*, *rajas* has demonstrated its power to produce the subject-object distinction that characterizes speech at its two lower levels. The formation of the *ahaṁkāra,* with its sense of egoity, provides for the overall sense of awareness, which, in its more individuated forms as mind and senses, forms the basis for the experiencing of epistemic curiosity. At the finite level of ego, mind, and senses, such an epistemic drive has been shown to provide both the desire to bring into self-awareness that hidden meaning *(artha)* of *sphoṭa* and the subsequent urge to express that revelation in uttered speech *(dhvani).* Now that the instinctive or dynamic basis for expression of *sphoṭa* has been described, the speaking act itself and its fully individuated manifestation of the *sphoṭa* as word-meaning *(artha)* and word-sound *(dhvani)* will be examined.

In Yoga psychology, perception may be thought of as being external or internal. External perception, of course, occurs through the sense organs. Internal perception is said to occur via the internal mental organ *(antaḥkaraṇa),* which assumes the threefold character of *buddhi, ahaṁkāra,* and *manas* accordingly as its functions differ. The *buddhi* functions as the discriminating, knowing intellect, the *ahaṁkāra* as providing perception with the ego sense of "mine," and the *manas* as the processing or liaison center between perceptive and motor activity. It should be noted here that in Yoga theory names such as *buddhi, ahaṁkāra,* and *manas* are used, not to refer to any kind of structural division within consciousness, but rather as an attempt to functionally describe the unified functioning of the whole *antaḥkaraṇa,* or mind.

In its *buddhi* function the *anataḥkaraṇa* contains the *saṁskāras* of both the word-meanings *(arthas)* and the word-sounds (*dhvanis* — vocalization patterns from previous lives). In its *ahaṁkāra* function the *antaḥkaraṇa* has the first awareness of the universal *artha,* or meaning, as its own cognition, and the concomitant awareness of the forming of that *artha* into inner speech, or *dhvani.* In the introspection of one's speaking act, this represents the cognitive birth of the earliest formulations in one's grasping of the whole idea, or *vākya sphoṭa.* The initial distinctions between *artha* and *dhvani* are therefore manifesting themselves.

At this stage the *manas* aspect of the *antaḥkaraṇa* is coordinating the concomitant developing vocalization patterns into internal thoughts in which the order of words is present. The *dhvani*-thoughts concomitant to the *artha* (of the *sphoṭa* in question) are psychologically composed by the interaction of the vibrant and highly charged *śabda tanmātra* with the organ of speech. The individuation of the *śabda tanmātra* into a particular *sphoṭa dhvani* manifestation occurs through the conjoint action of a variety of factors. The overall form of the *dhvani* is provided by the *artha* through its "magnetlike" attracting of the *tanmātra* into its (the *artha*'s) collateral *dhvani* pattern. But in order for the *śabda tanmātra* to be so structured, the speech organ acts as a variable filter through which the *tanmātra* is limited.[28] It is in this way that *vāsanās* of vocalization patterns from previous lives[29] instrumentally operate through the speech organ so that the speech organ and the electric vibrancy of the *śabda tanmātra* can together respond to the electromagnet-like pattern of the *artha* to produce the *dhvani*. Throughout all of this the *manas* is providing the psychomotor coordination for the complex cognitive activity involved.

The above-mentioned interpretation provides a practical psychological explanation, in terms of Yoga theory, of how the *sphoṭa* inherently present within the *buddhi* can express itself as *artha* and *dhvani* within individuated consciousness. In the analysis this far, however, *dhvani* is still at the level of thought or inner speech — corresponding to Bhartṛhari's *madhyamā vāk*. In addition to the organ of speech, the *prāṇa*, or breath, will also be involved — the psychomotor activities such as action of the muscles of the diaphragm in driving the *śabda tanmātra*, in its gross sound form, through the speech organ. In Yoga theory the individuating process is a continuum, so that even at the level of internal thought, the initial gross manifestations of *dhvani* will be present in a subtle fashion. Therefore to move to the final level of individuation requires only that the gross forms, already minutely present, receive further development. Speaking aloud requires only that the processes of one's thought-out sentences be given an increase of *prāṇa* until the gross, or *nāda*, articulation of the phonemes occurs.[30] In the case of written speech, a slightly different pattern of the *prāṇa* or psychomotor structuring (so as to include hand-eye coordination and a learned system of phonetic representation) is all that is required. This is Bhartṛhari's *vaikharī vāk* level of expression in which what is meant *(artha)* is produced as word-sound *(dhvani)* by the articulatory organs. Thus, interpreted according to Yoga psychology, the *Vākyapadīya* is seen to provide a logical and experienceable explanation of the speaking act.

IV *Psychological Processes in Hearing*

In the previous section the speaking act was described, showing how, according to Yoga psychology, the magnetlike action of the *artha* structured (or limited) the pervasive *śabda tanmātra* by filtering it through the inherent vocalization patterns (from *vāsanās* of word use in previous lives) of the speech organ so as to produce a *dhvani* or sound continuum, ranging from the subtle speech of inner thought to the gross articulation of the phonemes. Once articulated as configurations of gross atoms patterned by the psychomotor activities of the breath *(prāṇa)*, the phonemes continue to vibrate outward in expanding concentric circles from the speaker. The hearing act is initiated when the uttered phonemes in their concentric expansion as configurations of gross atoms (like waves moving outward when a stone is dropped into the water) strike against the hearing organ of the listener. Communication occurs, according to Bhartṛhari, when these sounds striking against the ear as uttered phonemes evoke in the mind of the listener a perception of the same *sphoṭa* from which the speaker began his utterance.

But exactly how do these discrete phoneme patterns striking against the ear psychologically function so as to evoke the partless *sphoṭa* inherently residing in each individual *buddhi*? On this question all Bhartṛhari offers are a few suggestions with regard to the function of *saṁskāras* and the general idea that the heard phonemes cognize the *sphoṭa* through a series of perceptions distorted by error — the *sphoṭa* perception following the hearing of the first phoneme having the highest error, and the *sphoṭa* perception following the hearing of the last phoneme the lowest error. Perhaps the most detailed psychological description of the process occurs in the *vṛtti*. "The sounds [phonemes], while they manifest the word *[sphoṭa]*, leave impression-seeds *[saṁskāras]* progressively clearer and conducive to the clear perception (of the word). Then, the final sound brings to the mind which has now attained maturity or a certain fitness by the awakening of the impressions of previous cognitions, the form of the word as coloured by itself."[31] But this is still a rather general analysis. Perhaps a more systematic interpretation can be obtained from Yoga psychology.

Fortunately, *Yoga Sūtra* III:17 deals with this exact question. The *sūtra* is stated in terms that seem to provide a very close parallel to those of the *sphoṭa* theory: "*śabda*" is used in the sense of the word-sound or *dhvani;* "*artha*" is interpreted — as in *sphoṭa* theory — to be the meaning or object; and "*pratyaya*" as the *ālambana* or support for the *śabda* and *artha* would seem to be very close to the *sphoṭa* of Bhartṛhari. In his *bhāṣya*, Vyāsa analyzes the hearing problem in terms almost identical to those of the *Vākyapadīya*.

. . . voice has its function [in uttering] only the [sounds of] syllables. And the organ-of-hearing has as its object only that [emission of air] which has been mutated into a sound [by contact with the eight places of articulation belonging to the vocal organ]. But it is a mental-process *(buddhi)* that grasps the word [as significant sound] by seizing the letter-sounds each in turn and binding them together [into one word]. Sounds-of-syllables *(varṇa)* do not naturally aid each other, for they cannot coexist at the same time. Not having attained-to-the-unity-of a word and not having [conveyed a definite meaning], they become audible *(āvis)* and they become inaudible *(tiras)*. Hence it is said that individually [letter-sounds] lack the nature of a word.[32]

Vyāsa thus ends up with the same problem as Bhartṛhari, namely, by what psychological mechanism do the ephemeral phonemes heard by the ear become bound together by the *buddhi* into a unity *(sphoṭa)* that manifests the meaning-whole?

Vyāsa begins the discussion of his solution to the problem by suggesting that each phoneme taken by itself is capable of standing for any meaning; it has universal application. But when a letter appears in combination with other letters, the preceding and following letters have the function of restricting or limiting the application of each letter to a particular meaning. Thus there are many uttered sounds, which by being placed in particular orders result in slightly different overall sounds — as determined by convention — and therefore are able to denote a certain meaning *(artha)*. For example, the literal sounds of *g*, *au*, and *ḥ*, possessed as they are of the potentiality of giving names to all objects *(arthas)*, denote in this particular order (*gauḥ*, "cow") the object that is possessed of udder, dewlap, and so on. Vācaspati adds the comment that a specific sonorous impression is thus established in the *antaḥkaraṇa*, as the hearing of the ordered utterance ceases. The specific sonorous impression that is evoked in the mind is the single image of the word *gauḥ*. This mental unity or *sphoṭa*, which is commonly called a word, has no parts or sequence within itself and reveals a meaning-object that is also one. The sequence of the uttered phonemes (as the last one is heard by the ear) reveals the one mental image of the *sphoṭa*. But what exactly is the psychological process by which this inner revelation of the one by the many heard phonemes takes place?

The solution offered by Vyāsa and Vācaspati is actually the logical counterpart of the process described in the last section, by which the *artha* of a particular *sphoṭa* resulted in the utterance of its particular vocalization of *śabda tanmātra* through the speech organ. The distinctive pattern of *dhvani* produced by the speech organ was described as being the resultant of the *saṁskāras* of speech patterns from previous lives and the "magnetlike" attraction of the *artha*. In the case of hearing, the particular phoneme sequence of the utterance approaches the ear as airwave modulations. The ear, because of its *sattvic*-dominated composition, responds to the magnetlike sound-wave pattern that was originally induced by the action of the *artha* on the *śabda tanmātra*. The *sattvic* aspect of the hearing organ thus begins with the hearing of the first phoneme, to approximate (vibrate in tune with) the total sound pattern sent out by the speaker. This sympathetic "vibration," which then travels throughout the consciousness of the hearer, induces maturation of the same *sphoṭa saṁskāra* series in the *buddhi* of the listener.[33] As the subsequent phonemes of the whole spoken pattern strike upon the ear, the sympathetic vibration induced within the hearer's *buddhi* more and more closely approximates the total sound pattern of the gross sound. With the hearing of the last phoneme, its particular "vibration" taken together with the "vibrations" of the preceding phonemes (still active within the *buddhi* by virtue of their self-induced *saṁskāras*) triggers a recognition of the inherent *sphoṭa* in the listener's *buddhi*.[34]

In this way a complete circle is established from speaker's *sphoṭa* to uttered phonemes to heard phonemes to perception of same *sphoṭa* within hearer. But if there is a completely closed circle from speaker's *sphoṭa* to hearer's *sphoṭa*, including both the *sattva*-dominated levels of the *buddhi* and the grosser levels of the external organs, and if consciousness has an inherent telos toward full revelation of the *sphoṭa* (as Īśvara's omniscience), then why is it that in our speech experience meaning seems to be conveyed in a mediate and often unclear fashion by the series of heard phonemes, rather than in a perfectly clear, immediate fashion by the unitary *sphoṭa*?

The reason for this obscuring of the circle of speech was previously seen, in the speaking act, to be due both to the finite nature of the individuated *manas* and speech organ (necessitating the expression of the noumenal whole in phenomenal parts), and to the obscuring of the meaning by the beginningless *avidyā*. The *avidyā*, or ignorance, referred to is the taking of the uttered letters and words produced by the organ of speech, *manas*, *prāṇa*, et cetera, to be the ultimate word. For these reasons the *sphoṭa* when spoken as a series of phonemes or sound vibrations is already considerably obscured and divided on its arrival at the hearer's ear. The hearer, through his own individuated consciousness, then has the task of trying to get back to the partless intuition of the *sphoṭa* from which the speaker began. The fact that the original *sphoṭa,* due to its pervasive existence in the *buddhitattva,* is already potentially present throughout the hearer's *buddhi sattva* (and its individuations into *ahaṁkāra, manas,* and organ of hearing) paves the way for its recognition. And as was the case in the speaking act, *saṁskāras* from our language-use in previous lives pervade the *manas* and the hearing organ so that the natural correlation between a sound pattern of uttered phonemes and its intended *artha* has become intensified (through usage in accordance with the consensus of the elders or *saṅketa*).[35]

Although this *saṅketa* intensification of the natural correlation has the positive function of helping the hearer to perceive the *sphoṭa* intended by the speaker, it has at the same time an obscuring *(avidyā)* effect described by both Bhartṛhari and Vyāsa as *adhyāsa,* or superimposition. Bhartṛhari says that the conventional understanding of the uttered words as being one with the meaning is a case of *adhyāsa.*[36] The meaning whole is superimposed upon the parts but the obscuring *avidya* of *vaikharī* speech is such that the true direction of the superimposition is not realized and the *ālambana* or ground of the hearing is taken to be the gross sound pattern rather than the *sphoṭa.* Vyāsa says that our taking of the uttered and heard phoneme word pattern to be something real in itself is a result of common understanding *(sampratipatti).* "It is owing to our knowing what this [word] means in accordance with conventional-usage that we attempt to divide it [into sounds of syllables]."[37] Vācaspati shows that psychologically the expression of the word is really a single *vṛtti* or effort of articulation (as is evidenced by the particular order and unity that makes the utterance of r-a-s-a completely distinct from the word s-a-r-a). The listener also distinguishes between these two words in that the hearing of each word-whole is also done by a functional whole or single consciousness state in spite of the fact that conventional usage and grammatical analysis seem to suggest a series of single states, one for each letter.[38] Vyāsa explains psychologically the conventional error as a result of the mutual superimposition or mixing up in the mind of the uttered sounds *(śabda),* the meaning *(artha),* and the *ālambana pratyaya (sphoṭa).*

Before describing the detailed analysis of this mixed-up state of *vaikharī* hearing, brief note will be taken of the way in which Yoga psychology, in agreement with the *Vākyapadīya,* interprets the single consciousness state evoked in the hearing of the word as being ultimately the sentence *sphoṭa* rather than word *sphoṭa*. In all perceived words, says Vyāsa, there is the inherent hearing of the *vākya-sphoṭa*, or unitary sentence meaning. If the word "tree" is uttered the single hearing effort inherently includes within it the verb "is" *(asti)* since no intended meaning *(artha)* can lack existence. Thus the single consciousness state within the listener is the *vākya sphoṭa* "It is a tree." Similarly in the case of the utterance of a single word that is a verb (e.g., "cooks"), the single hearing effort of the listener perceives the agent and any other expansions required as being present in *vākya sphoṭa* (e.g., "Chaitra cooks rice in the vessel on the fire").[39] In *Yoga Sūtra* III:17, with its commentaries, we have therefore found a faithful psychological interpretation of Bhartṛhari's thesis that the sentence-meaning is the indivisible unit of speech *(vākya-sphoṭa)*, and that ultimately it is the only real *(satya)*.[40] The above Yoga interpretation of the hearing event has also outlined the very mixing together of *dhvani*, *artha*, and *sphoṭa* that Bhartṛhari has defined as *vāk* at the *vaikharī*, or gross, level.

In *Yoga Sūtra* I:42 we find an even more detailed psychological analysis of *vaikharī vāk*. Here the same technical terms "*śabda*" and "*artha*" are used (corresponding to the *sphoṭa* "*dhvani*" and "*artha*"), but instead of "*pratyaya*" the word "*jñāna*" is employed to refer to the idea or "*sphoṭa*." These three are described by Patañjali as being mixed up or superimposed on one another in various predicate relations *(vikalpas)* so that the intended meaning of the word is not clearly seen. In line with *sphoṭa* theory, Vācaspati notes that these predicate relations among *śabda*, *artha*, and *jñāna* represent the diversity that there is in one thing, and the identity that there is in diverse things. For example, in *vaikharī* speech a hearer of the sound pattern "cow" finds, on Yogic introspection, that three possibilities present themselves: (1) there is a predicate relation in which the *śabda* and *jñāna* are dominated and appropriated by the *artha* "cow"; (2) there is a predicate relation in which *jñāna* and *artha* are dominated and appropriated by the *śabda* "cow"; and (3) there is a predicate relation in which *śabda* and *artha* are dominated and appropriated by the *jñāna* "cow."

Vyāsa finds that the psychological cause of this mixed-up perception of the true meaning is twofold. On the one hand, there is the distortion caused by the *saṁskāras* of *saṅketa* (conventional word use in previous lives), discussed above, and resulting in the universally experienced error of type (2) *vikalpa*. On the other hand, there are the cognitive inferences *(anumānas)* based upon the *artha* — made by one's own imaginative thinking or heard from the traditional schools of thought *(darśanas)*. Such *anumāna*-dominated hearing would seem to be an error of type (3) with the erroneous element being the "slanting" or "coloring" given the *sphoṭa* by the doctrinal presuppositions of the particular *darśana* heard. Although not elucidated by either Vyāsa or Vācaspati, the type (1) situation, in which the *artha* predominates, would seem to be closest to true perception yet still erroneous due to its predicate relations with the other two types. Such predicate relations would be experienced because of the finite structural individuations of consciousness through which the speech is necessarily heard (i.e., the organ of hearing, *manas, prāṇa, śabda-tanmātra,* etc.) in ordinary states of consciousness. These types of *vikalpa* are therefore shown to be the psychological processes producing the high error perception that characterizes the verbal, or *vaikharī,* level of hearing. To such high-error-level perception Yoga applies the technical term *savitarkā,* which means indistinct concentration *(samādhi)* of the consciousness.

As the concentrated perception of the word is gradually purified or freed from memory *(saṅketa),* and the predicate relations of inference *(anumāna),* the consciousness state approaches what Bhartṛhari calls *madhyamā vāk.* This is the inner hearing aspect of the complete communication circle the *sphoṭa* forms in its "vibratory movement" from the *buddhi* of the speaker to the *buddhi* of the hearer. In the *Vākyapadīya* commentaries it is described as having the *ahaṁkāra,* or ego, as its only substratum and having sequence present but only in a very subtle fashion. *Dhvani* and *artha* are still distinct and the order of words is present. Although sequence or predicate relations are suppressed, they are said to be accompanied by a distinct functioning of *prāṇa.*[41] Whereas in the speaking act the psychomotor *prāṇa,* or breath, functions served to individuate the *sphoṭa* pattern through the coordination of the *śabda-tanmātra* and vocal organ, the process is reversed in hearing with *prāṇa* and *manas* working to reintegrate the gross differentiations of the *sphoṭa* pattern at the ear level into the less differentiated vibration patterns of the *śabda tanmātra, manas,* and *ahaṁkāra.* As the more integrated heights of *madhyamā vāk* are realized, the overall preponderance of *sattva* in the *sphoṭa* vibration pattern correspondingly increases until a clearer perception of the unified *sphoṭa* occurs.

A kind of idealized or criterion description of *madhyamā* in its purest form is offered by the Yoga analysis of *savicāra*, or meditative, *samādhi*.[42] In *savicāra* the intensity of concentration is such that the *sattva* is so transparent that the *artha*, or true meaning, of the given *sphoṭa* stands revealed in the mind *(antaḥkāraṇa)* with little distortion or obscuration. On the subjective *(sattva)* side the distortion decreases as the integration of the heard *sphoṭa* moves from the high *rajas*–low *sattva* ratio of the *manas* and senses to the low *rajas*–high *sattva* ratio of the *ahaṁkāra*. On the objective *(tamas)* side, the overall obscuration of the *sphoṭa*-patterned consciousness state decreases as the *rajas* activation of the *śabda tanmātra* becomes less and less until the state of pure potential is approached. Vyāsa describes the *savicāra* state as being composed of the essences of all the gross particularizations of the *sphoṭa* pattern. Vācaspati notes that just as the gross atoms (at the *vaikharī* level) are patterned by the *manas* and *prāṇa* into a whole by a single effort of consciousness, so also in the *savicāra* state the subtle electronlike *tanmātras* are patterned by the *prāṇa* (although less *prāṇa* than at the *vaikharī* level) and the *antaḥkaraṇa* into the same whole by a single effort of consciousness.

The distortions still found at the *savicāra* level of inner hearing include notions of time, place, and causation. But characteristics associated with the hearing of the gross sound (dialect, speed of speaking, emotional colorations by voice timbre, etc.) will have virtually all dropped away in the *savicāra citta*. The influence of *saṅketa saṁskāras* (memory traces of conventional word usage), while not entirely absent, will be greatly reduced. Far more powerful will be the intensifying of the *artha* aspect of the *sattva citta* due to magnetlike attraction exerted by the pure *saṁskāra* series of the *buddhitattva sphoṭa* upon the "approaching" and integrating manifestation of the *sphoṭa* pattern within the listener's consciousness.

Now, although the above Yoga analysis provides a psychological description of the meditative, or *madhyamā, vāk* and satisfies the primary task of the psychological interpretation, the secondary question of how one's ordinary *vaikharī* perception of *vāk*, which is in the confused *savitarkā* state of consciousness, can be raised to a higher level has yet to be answered. This second answer is especially important if Bhartṛhari is correct in his observation that in many people, owing to poor word usage in their previous lives, the divine *vāk* (in its pristine state as the pure *saṁskāra* series of Īśvara's *sattva*) has become badly mixed up with corrupt word forms. And since both the divine and the corrupt forms are being handed down to us in our inherent *vāsanās*, some means of purifying one's *vāk* is required in order to avoid being trapped forever at the *vaikharī* level.[43] Should this happen, not only would we be prevented from the earthly happiness and merit that result from the correct use of words, but we would also suffer the endless pain engendered by never being able to achieve the ultimate bliss of *mokṣa*, which comes from the realization of oneness with *Śabdabrahman*. Bhartṛhari clearly assumes the practical possibility of such a purification of one's *vāk*. Although he does not describe the process required, he technically designates it as *śabdapūrvayoga*.

V Śabdapūrvayoga *as Interpreted by the* Yoga Sūtras

If one is fortunate enough to be born as a sage, as a result of the cumulative effect of good word use in previous lives, little more than continued practice of *vairāgya* (the turning away of the mind from all forms of worldly attachment) and *abhyāsa* (the habitual steadying of the mind in concentration upon the Vedic *sphoṭa*) is required to ensure ascent to *Śabdabrahman*.[44] But before the ordinary person can attempt such advanced *vairāgya* and *abhyāsa*, his habitually distracted state of mind, owing to lack of concentration and the obscuring habit patterns of bad word usage *(vāsanās)*, must be overcome. To this end the *Yoga Sūtras* offer some specific techniques that may well have been what Bhartṛhari had in mind as *śabdapūrvayoga*. According to Vyāsa these Yoga techniques function simply by removing the obstacles (i.e., the *vāsanās*, or habit patterns, of bad word usage) that are preventing consciousness from flowing toward *mokṣa* under the motive force of its own inherent teleology. Yoga psychology maintains that in itself consciousness *(citta)* is always attempting to move toward *mokṣa*. Therefore, all that the specific Yoga techniques do is to remove the obstructions within the mind, and consciousness then passes naturally into the state of *mokṣa*.[45]

In *Yoga Sūtra* II:29 Patañjali lists eight Yoga techniques or practices *(yogāṅgas)*. They are *yama*, or restraints; *niyama*, or disciplines; *āsanas*, or body postures; *prāṇāyāma*, or regulation of breath; *pratyāhāra*, or freedom of the mind from sensory domination by external objects; *dhāraṇā*, or concentration; *dhyāna*, or Yogic meditation; and *samādhi*, or trance. These classic Yoga disciplines will be examined in relation to Bhartṛhari's concept of *śabdapūrvayoga*.

Although Patañjali lists five *yamas*, or self-restraints, which when practiced will remove the gross impurities obstructing the perception of *sphoṭa* in ordinary minds, from the point of view of *śabdapūrvayoga* it is the discipline of *satya,* or truthfulness, that commands special attention. *Satya* is the conformity of one's speech and mind *(citta vṛtti)* with the thing itself. Word and thought must conform with the facts that have been seen, heard, and inferred. Vyāsa points out that since the function of speech is to communicate one's understanding to others, therefore it must contain no illusion nor should it create illusion in others if it is true speech *(vāk).* This *vāk* is for the benefit of all beings, but not for their injury. In this regard, Manu is quoted: "Utter what is beneficial to others; do not utter what is true but injurous to others . . . therefore, after careful enquiry one should speak the truth which will be beneficial to all beings."[46]

In addition to speaking the truth, there are the powerful cleansing and mind-controlling practices of *svādhyāya. Svādhyāya,* or concentrated study, includes both the recital of passages of scripture, and the repetition of *mantras* such as AUM. "Study" here implies not only reading the scripture for its rational content, but also saying it meditatively. Without any attempt at rational analysis, one simply repeats the verse over and over so as to let the revelatory power inherent within it work upon one's consciousness. In addition to repeating scriptural verses in this fashion, one should also chant the sacred syllable AUM. The more one repeats such verbalizations of the *ṛṣis,* the more power they have to break through the veiling ignorance of one's mind so as to evoke or reveal the Divine Word that is within. In terms of the "energy vibration" analogy used previously to describe the hearing of the spoken word, the process would be as follows. Concentrated repetitions reinforce the "*sattvic* vibrations," which the spoken Vedic words induce within the mental organ *(antaḥkaraṇa),* resulting in a powerful sympathetic "vibration" deep within the *paśyantī,* or highest level of consciousness, until the pure *sphoṭa* is revealed in a flash of insight.

This conception of study aims at freeing one's mind of obstructions and distractions and simply allowing the power of the Divine Word to work within one's consciousness. Rather than doing the thinking and revealing the truth by one's own effort, as is the case in rational analysis, here one is quieting one's own thinking and allowing the Divine Word, which is both immanent within consciousness and externally presented as the authoritative scriptural revelation, itself to speak. While this kind of "study" until recently was virtually unknown in modern Western life, it was present in the medieval West and is currently being rediscovered in contemporary movements such as Transcendental Meditation and the new student interest in Judaeo-Christian Monastic Contemplation.[47]

As *vāk* (including both external speaking and internal thinking) becomes more meditative, there is a reduction in all gross psychomotor activity.[48] In Yoga this internalization of concentration is fostered by the three aids of body postures *(āsanas)*, breath control *(prāṇāyāma)*, and withdrawal of senses *(pratyahāra)*. The taking up of a stable posture, or *āsana*, is not complete until it can be maintained without any mental effort — so that all possible movements of the body are restrained, thus freeing consciousness from gross *prāṇa* activity and assisting in stabilizing the subtle *prāṇa* required for *madhyamā vāk*.[49] A practical criterion is given whereby the Yogin can test himself. Mastery of *āsanas* is indicated when the Yogin can remain unaffected by the pairs of opposites, such as heat and cold, while meditating upon his verse, or *mantra*.[50]

As another aid to *śabdapūrvayoga*, the devotee must further control the *vaikharī*, or ordinary expression of speech and thought, by the practice of *prāṇāyāma* (controlled respiration). *Prāṇāyāma* is defined as the pause that comes after each deep inhalation and each deep exhalation. When practiced in conjunction with *āsana*, a high degree of external stability and control is achieved over involvements of consciousness in the gross sequences that characterize the manifestation of *vakharī vāk*. As Bhartṛhari observes, at the *madhyamā* level the cognition of *vāk* is chiefly associated with the internal mental organ *(antaḥkaraṇa)* and not with the organs of gross articulation or hearing, and therefore the kind of *prāṇa* required is very subtle. By using various specified methods of measurement, the Yogin can determine the length of pauses he is achieving and compare them against the established standards of *mātrā*, or instant (the time taken to snap the fingers after turning the hand over the knee three times), first or mild *udghāta* (thirty-six such *mātrās*), second or moderate *udghāta* (first *udghāta* doubled), and third or intense *udghāta* (first *udghāta* tripled). A special fourth kind of *prāṇāyāma* is achieved by applying the Yogic psychological principle of counteracting unwanted tendencies by the forceful practice of their opposites. In this case, the breath is drawn in forcibly when it has a tendency to go out, and thrown out forcibly when it has a tendency to go in. By such negative practice plus the three easier kinds of restraint, breathing becomes so inhibited that it may virtually cease for long periods. The purpose of this practice is said to be the destruction of the impurities (such as delusions caused by traces of corrupt word usage) from consciousness until it becomes so luminous or *sattvic* that clear perception of the *sphoṭa* becomes possible.[51] Only then is the mind judged to be truly fit for *dhāraṇā*, or "fixed concentration." As Eliade observes, a remark of Bhoja states clearly the underlying principle: "All the functions of the organs being preceded by that of respiration — there being always a connection between respiration and consciousness in their respective functions — respiration, when all the functions of the organs are suspended, realizes concentration of consciousness on a single object."[52] This principle — that there is a direct connection between respiration and mental states — is fundamental for Yoga.

A further aid to turning the flow of consciousness away from the gross manifestations of uttered speech and toward the *sphoṭa*'s internal *artha* (meaning) aspect is the Yoga practice of *pratyāhāra*. *Pratyāhāra* is defined as the disciplined withdrawal of the senses from their preoccupation with external manifestations so as to become focused with all of consciousness in single-pointed contemplation of the internal *artha*. Vyāsa offers the analogy that, just as when the king bee (queen bee in the West) settles down all the other bees follow, so, when consciousness is restricted and concentrated the sense organs are also withdrawn and concentrated. This is *pratyāhāra*, which, along with the practice of *āsanas* and *prāṇāyāma*, results in control over the *vaikharī*, or external expression of *vāk*.

In the aforementioned discussion it has been shown how the practices detailed by the *Yoga Sūtras* purify consciousness to the level of single-pointedness *(ekāgratā)*. This Yoga analysis would seem to correspond with Bhartṛhari's basic requirements for *śabdapūrvayoga* — the rising above the gross expression of *prāṇa* and the cutting of the knots that bring about the differentiation of *vāk*.[53]

The last three practices, described as the direct aids to Yoga, are: *dhāraṇā*, or fixed concentration; *dhyāna*, or Yogic meditation; and *samādhi*, or trance contemplation. They represent three stages of the same process; which is given the technical name *saṁyama* (perfected contemplation).[54] For the practice of *śabdapūrvayoga*, *dhāraṇā* would be the fixed concentration of consciousness upon the *artha*, or meaning, of the *sphoṭa*. Dasgupta helpfully clarifies the necessary relationship between *dhāraṇā* and *pratyāhāra* (withdrawal of senses). *Dhāraṇā* and *pratyāhāra* must be practiced together as conjoint means for achieving the same end. *Dhāraṇā* without *pratyāhāra* or *pratyāhāra* without *dhāraṇā* would both be fruitless endeavors.[55] Vijñāna Bhikṣu suggests that in terms of elapsed time, *dhāraṇā* must last as long as twelve *prāṇāyāmas*.[56]

Dhyāna is the continuance or uninterrupted flow of fixed concentration upon *artha* in the stream of consciousness.[57] It is the continuation of the mental effort to clearly perceive the *sphoṭa.* Vijñāna Bhikṣu indicates that in terms of elapsed time, *dhyāna* may be thought of as lasting as long as twelve *dharaṇās* — which would equal one hundred forty-four *prāṇāyāmas.* Mastery at this *madhyamā* level of *vāk* is indicated by the lack of intrusion of any other mental state *(citta-vṛtti)* during this period of meditation.

Samādhi, or trance contemplation, occurs when the *dhyāna* loses its subject-object distinction. As Vyāsa puts it, "when fixed concentration shines forth only in the form of the object being contemplated and empty of all duality, that is *samādhi.*[58] Vācaspati further clarifies the point as follows. A *kalpanā* or two-termed-relation is a distinction between the concentration and the object upon which it is fixed. *Dhāraṇā* and *dhyāna* exhibit such subject-object distinction. However, all duality is absent in *samādhi,* where the mind has fused itself with or become one with the object. In this state there is no self-awareness but only a direct intuition — knowing by becoming one with the object. For *śabdapūrvayoga* this would mark the transition from the dualistic experience of *sphoṭa* as *dhvani* and *artha* — grossly manifested at the *vaikharī* level and subtly manifested at the *madhyamā* level — to the unitary perception of the *sphoṭa,* which characterizes the *pratibhā* of the *paśyantī* level of *vāk.* It is this *paśyantī* state of *sphoṭa samādhi* that provides the psychological process by which the *śabda* devotee may make his ascent toward *mokṣa* — union with *Śabdabrahman.* At the lower levels of *vaikharī* and *madhyamā,* however, the correct use of words through practices such as *satya* helps to produce spiritual merit *(dharma),* which makes the attainment of happiness here and beyond certain. But for the ultimate end, correct usage alone is not enough. When the lower practices *(yogāṅgas)* are combined with the higher *samādhi* forms, *śabdapūrvayoga* then opens the way to the ultimate end, and the realization of *mokṣa.*

Samādhi is the goal of the *śabdapūrvayoga* and all the Yoga practices must work together for its achievement. It cannot be achieved unless, as the Yogin tries to withdraw his senses and focus his mind, potential obstructions arising from the unsteadiness of the body and the mind are controlled by *āsana* and *prāṇāyāma.* And then only gradually, through the steadying of the mind on one *sphoṭa,* does consciousness *(citta)* begin to flow evenly without any disruption. Finally, the mind even ceases to think that it is thinking the *sphoṭa* itself. Although, theoretically, the last three stages are separated,

Patañjali makes clear that in practice *dhāraṇā*, *dhyāna*, and *samādhi* are all part of the same process of which the last one is perfection. Success is indicated by the shining forth of *prajñā* (insight or direct perception of the *sphoṭa)*, and is the *paśyantī* level of *vāk*.[59]

Throughout the *Vākyapadīya* analysis of the levels of *vāk*, it seems clear that Bhartṛhari's concept is that these levels are heuristic levels on a contiuuum rather than discrete hierarchial stages. The same sort of heuristic continuum is also envisaged in the Yoga analysis of the various levels of *samādhi*.[60] This means that within the *paśyantī pratibhā* there will be degrees of clearness in the unitary perception of *sphoṭa*. It is fitting, therefore, that in the *Yoga Sūtras*, when *samādhi* is being analyzed in its nondualistic or *pratibhā* state, two qualities of *prajñā* are described: *nirvitarka*, or gross *pratibhā* of the *sphoṭa*, and *nirvicāra*, or subtle *pratibhā* of the *sphoṭa*.

Nirvitarka, or gross perception of the *sphoṭa*, occurs when the *samādhi* is freed from memory, the conventional usage of *śabda*, and the predicate relations of *jñāna* by inference or association, allowing the thing-itself *(svarūpa)* to shine forth in itself alone. In this stage the *svarūpa (sphoṭa)* is directly intuited as having just that form which it has in itself and nothing more. *Citta* has become one with the object so that the object no longer appears as an object of consciousness.[61] The duality of subject and object is overcome, leaving only the steady transformation of *citta* in the form of the object of its contemplation. Here the *samādhi* knowledge or *prajñā* is an outgrowth from the *savitarka samādhi*. It is of the grosser *vaikharī* manifestation of the *sphoṭa* as perceived in its formal pattern or unity through the senses.

Nirvicāra samādhi develops naturally from the meditative concentration *(savicāra)* that was previously found to characterize *madhyamā vāk*. When, by constant *śabdapūrvayoga*, the mind becomes so much identified with the subtle aspects of the *savicāra samādhi* that notions of time, place, and causality disappear, and the *antaḥkaraṇa* becomes one with the *sattvic sphoṭa*, that is *nirvicāra*.[62] In this *samādhi* state the *śabda* Yogin's *citta* becomes so purified that the *prajñā* obtained is perfectly pure and considered to be absolute knowledge of the *sphoṭa*. It is the final clear no-error perception of the *sphoṭa* and is at the opposite end of the hearer's continuum from the high-error initial experiences of the phonemes at the *vaikharī* level. This *nirvicāra samādhi*, which is Patañjali's highest *samprajñāta* or "seeded" stage, seems equivalent to Bhartṛhari's *viśiṣṭopahita*, or highest *pratibhā*.[63] It is the same process by which the *ṛṣis* cognize the Vedas, but, unlike the more ordinary *śabda* Yogin, the great sages are said to have been able to directly perceive the noumenal *sphoṭa* without having to go through the process of errors. The *prajñā*, or knowledge revealed by the direct perception of the *sphoṭa*, is described as having a twofold character: (1) it gives the special or true knowledge of the word, and (2) it gives the power to act in accordance with that knowledge.[64] It is through both of these capacities that the *pratibhā* perception of *sphoṭa* provides the means for *mokṣa* realization. From the Yoga viewpoint, this situation is described in a more technical psychological fashion, as follows. When the *śabda* Yogin remains in the concentrated insight of the *nirvicāra* state, the ongoing impact of this insight *(prajñā)* upon consciousness effectively restricts the emergence of any remaining negative *saṁskāras*. By such *śabdapūrvayoga*, any remaining obstacles are removed and the inherent telos within consciousness itself finds *mokṣa* — oneness with *Śabdabrahman*.

CHAPTER 4

Bhartṛhari's Dhvani *as Central to Indian Aesthetics*

BHARTṚHARI'S *Vākyapadīya* is at once a textbook of Sanskrit grammar, a complete philosophy of language, a theology, and a practical spiritual discipline for the attainment of *mokṣa*. In addition to all this, the *Vākyapadīya*, in its concept of the evocative power of word sound *(dhvani)*, appears to have exerted a strong influence in the field of Indian aesthetics.

I Dvani: *A Central Notion in Indian Aesthetics*

Standard histories of Indian aesthetics describe *dhvani*, or suggestion, as a central notion.[1] The agreed authoritative definition of *dhvani* is given within the context of poetics by Anandavardhana as follows: "That kind of poetry wherein either the (conventional) meaning or the (conventional) word renders itself or its meaning secondary (respectively) and suggests the implied meaning, is designated by the learned as DHVANI or 'suggestive poetry.' "[2] The earliest example of *dhvani* is usually taken from Vālmīki's *Rāmāyana*; the particular incident runs as follows. Once Vālmīki went to the river for his midday bath. While walking in the beautiful forest, he came upon a pair of birds (called *krauñca*) engaged in the act of mating. As Vālmīki stood gazing at this sight an arrow came from behind, killing the male bird. The shock of this terrible turn of events changed the female's joyous twitter into a terrified shriek. Vālmīki was deeply moved by her plight. He completely forgot himself and for a moment fully identified with the helpless female bird. Then from his lips burst forth a poetic expression of grief: "Hunter, may you never get any peace. You have killed one of the pair of krauñcas in the state of infatuation with love."[3] This spontaneous outpouring is said to be the first poetic expression in classical Sanskrit, as well as the first example of *dhvani*. K. C. Pandey analyzes the poetic expression as follows:

[Vāmīki] speaks not as Vālmīki, but as the female Krauñca universalized. He views the situation as the latter. He, therefore, experiences the loss of what was the dearest and most precious. This has meant to him the irrecoverable loss of peace of mind. He looks upon the hunter as the author of his perpetual grief. He feels his helplessness against the enemy. And, therefore, in the characteristic manner of a widowed woman [whose husband has been senselessly murdered], he curses the hunter with a lot very much worse than his own.[4]

In Indian aesthetics this is considered inspired poetry because of the deep feeling of grief that the words in their rhyme, meter, juxtaposition, and so forth, arouse. It is *dhvani* because the expression of grief is accomplished without the use of the word "grief" or any of its synonyms. The feeling is too deep, intense, and universal to be directly expressed in conventional words — it can only be evoked or suggested indirectly, and this is the notion of *dhvani* in aesthetics. Prior to this aesthetics usage, however, the notion of *dhvani* had been carefully formulated by Bhartṛhari in his *Vākyapadīya*.

II *Bhartṛhari's* Dhvani *as Developed by the Literary Critics*

It is in the *Vākyapadīya*, Bhartṛhari's great work on the philosophy of language, that the term *dhvani* appears. The commentary on *kānda* I, *kārikā* 5, states that the Veda though One has been put into a diversity of poems or hymns *(dhvanis)* by the *ṛṣis*. Although the various manifestations of the one Veda may vary in *dhvani* (form and style of expression) from poet to poet and from region to region, it is the same *dharma*, or truth, that is being voiced throughout.[5] This is the basic model upon which Bhartṛhari constructs his theory of language. The central or essential idea of the poem is a given that is inherently present in the poet's consciousness (and the consciousness of everyone else). At the first moment of its revelation the poet is completely caught up into this unitary idea, or *sphoṭa*, as Bhartṛhari calls it. But then as he starts to examine the idea with an eye to its communication, he has withdrawn himself from the first intimate unity with the idea, symbol, or inspiration itself, and now experiences it in a twofold fashion. On the one hand there is its objective meaning, which he is seeking to communicate, and on the other are the words and phrases he will utter. Further on in the *Vākyapadīya*[6] Bhartṛhari provides a technical analysis, which could be diagramed as follows:

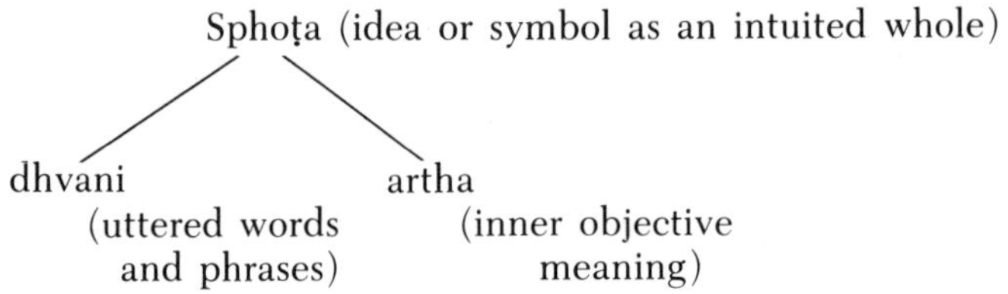

For Bhartṛhari the sentence, play, poem, essay, or book taken as a meaning-whole is the *sphoṭa*. The technical term *sphoṭa* is difficult to translate into English. Sometimes the word "symbol" is used for *sphoṭa*, while at other times the Greek conception of *logos* and the Platonic notion of the innate idea have been suggested as approximating *sphoṭa*. In his *Sphoṭavāda*, Nāgeśa Bhaṭṭa describes *sphoṭa* in two ways: as that from which the meaning bursts or shines forth; and as an entity that is manifested by the spoken letters or sounds.[7] The *sphoṭa* may thus be thought of as a kind of two-sided coin. On the one side it is manifested by the uttered sounds, and on the other side it simultaneously reveals the inner meaning. In a more philosophic sense, *sphoṭa* may be described as the transcendent ground in which the spoken syllables and conveyed meaning find themselves united.

Bhartṛhari's theory seems to fit quite well when it is illustrated with reference to one's experience of poetry. Take, for example, the word "love," which Bhartṛhari would call a *sphoṭa*. Although the meaning of the word "love" ultimately may be experienced as a unitary intuition, the communication of that insightful knowledge may well require the employment of a variety of suggestive poetic expressions:

> Let me not to the marriage of true minds
> Admit impediments. Love is not love
> Which alters when it alteration finds,
> Or bends with the remover to remove:
> O, No! it is an ever-fixed mark,
> That looks on tempests, and is never shaken;
> It is the star to every wandering bark,
> Whose worth's unknown, although his height be taken.
> Love's not Time's fool, though rosy lips and cheeks
> Within his bending sickle's compass come;
> Love alters not with his brief hours and weeks,
> But bears it out even to the edge of doom.

> If this be error and upon me prov'd,
> I never writ, nor no man ever lov'd.[8]

In this sonnet, Shakespeare, through the use of his poetic imagination, composes a variety of expressions that when uttered manifest in the listener's mind an intuitive perception of the word-symbol "love" and its meaning. Different people may experience the manifestations of the unitary word-meaning differently. For some it may come as a sudden flash of intuition, full-blown in its development. Others, however, may experience a gradual and progressive revelation through repeated exposures to suggestive poetic phrases. In Bhartṛhari's view, the word-*sphoṭa* "love" is a given, unitary and eternal in nature, but, as the history of literature, religion, and marital relations demonstrates, a given requiring many imperfectly suggestive expressions before its meaning is fully grasped or intuitively realized in one's mind. It is the uttered expression, which Bhartṛhari called *dhvani*, that comes to occupy a central place in Indian aesthetics and receives further development in the hands of the literary critics.

The utterance "Love is unalterable, eternal, and matchless and ageless" would likely qualify, according to the grammarians, as a *dhvani* sequence serving to manifest the word-*sphoṭa* "love." For Indian aesthetics, however, something more is needed before such an external expression could be considered a full revelation of the inner word meaning, and therefore worthy of being called *dhvani*. That "something more" would be the kind of poetic expression encountered in Shakespeare's sonnet. The hallmark of such *dhvani* or greatness of poetic expression is that in it "the symbolic surpasses all the poetic elements in point of strikingness and shines in its full splendor as the cynosure of all minds."[9] Rather than just a dry philosophic making-present of the word-meaning, the champion of Indian aesthetics claims for *dhvani* a particular excellence in revelatory experience. In the poetic experience of *dhvani* the transcendental function of suggestion removes the primordial veil of ignorance from our minds and thereby allows the bliss associated with the discovery of true meaning to be experienced.

Among the literary critics of India, Anandavardhana seems to have been the first to make use of Bhartṛhari's notion of *dhvani*. It is *kārikā* 47 of *kānda* I that directly provides the basis for interpreting *dhvani* in terms of "suggestion." There Bhartṛhari says it is the spoken words that suggest the inner meaning *(artha)* and eventually evoke the unified *sphoṭa.*[10] Anandavardhana picks up the notion of *dhvani* as the suggestive power of the spoken words, but also uses *dhvani* to refer to the thing suggested, namely, the principle poetic mood or meaning.[11] Each of these usages will be examined in turn.

Dhvani refers to the suggestive function *(vyañjanā)* of the words and phrases of the poem or drama. But whereas for Bhartṛhari it is the conventional inner meaning, or *artha*, that is called forth, Anandavardhana specializes the notion of *dhvani* so that it refers to the specific poetic sense rather than the ordinary meaning. The traditional example offered is the phrase "a hamlet on the Ganges." What is meant here is more than just the conventional meanings of the individual words since that would result in a house in the middle of the river Ganges. Therefore the secondary *(lakṣaṇā)* sense of a house on the bank of the Ganges is understood. But if the phrase were part of a poem, yet another level of meaning would be involved. The words "a hamlet on the Ganges" would suggest, not just a house on the riverbank, but a house that, because of its proximity to the Ganges, is cool, pure, and holy. Of course all this could be spelled out word for word, but then it would lose its special poetic sense. Sankaran clearly analyzes this distinction:

> This idea of the coolness and sanctity of the hamlet is delightful when suggested from "a hamlet on the Ganges," but it is not so when understood expressly from "a hamlet on the bank of the Ganges is very cool and holy"; for in getting at the idea there is in the former a peculiar exercise to the mind which only an intellectual man can take, and it delights him, while in the latter this is totally absent. The Dhvani school holds that the presence of the suggested idea above the express sense distinguishes poetry from ordinary language.[12]

The presence of a larger suggested sense (inclusive of idea, mood, and mystic intuition) over and above the primary *(abhidhā)* and secondary *(lakṣaṇā)* meanings makes the passage poetry rather than ordinary language.

Sankaran provides an example from the great Indian poet Daṇḍin to further clarify this distinction: "Depart my dear! if thou dost, then may thy paths be safe! Let me also be born again in that place whither thou wouldst be gone" (Daṇḍin, *Kāvyādarśa* II:141). The verse is spoken by a lady to her beloved on the eve of his departure on a long journey. In its conventional or primary meanings the verse simply wishes the lover a happy journey and says that she wishes to be reborn in the place where her lover is going. This is the exact meaning of the words. But the poetic sense suggests much more. By desiring rebirth in the land to which her beloved is going, she is suggesting that he should not leave for if he does she will die from the pain of their separation. To put it very plainly she could have said, "My dear, I love you intensely; so do not go. If you do, I will certainly commit suicide."[13] But in this form no poetic feeling, none of the subtle aesthetic sense of the poetic passage is evoked. Here the term *dhvani* refers to the special suggestive function *(vyañjanā)* of the poetic phrases.

But Anandavardhana also uses *dhvani* to refer to the total mood and/or idea that is suggested. In the example of the lady and her beloved both an idea *(artha)* and a dominant mood *(rasa)* are evoked by the suggestive power of the poetry. The idea, that the beloved should not depart, and the mood of intense love in the face of impending separation are both termed *dhvani*. With reference to Bhartṛhari's language model, this usage would seem to parallel the notion of *sphoṭa* as the meaning-whole manifested by the spoken words *(dhvanis)*. Thus we see that Anandavardhana expanded Bhartṛhari's usage of *dhvani*, which referred to the manifested sounds, to include the *artha* and *sphoṭa* as well. But whereas Bhartṛhari's *sphoṭa* connoted more the abstract unitary idea, Anandavardhana's *dhvani*, as the end poetic experience, includes an emphasis on the aesthetic feeling or mood as well as the unitary idea. These added aspects that distinguish Anandavardhana's *dhvani* from Bhartṛhari's *sphoṭa* occur as a direct result of the poetic rather than the ordinary way of speaking.[14]

This use of *dhvani* to refer to the aesthetic mood or feeling itself also allowed Anandavardhana to subsume the older notion of *rasa* under *dhvani*. Some centuries earlier, possibly around the sixth century A.D., Bharata in his *Nāṭyaśāstra* had established *rasa* as the "soul" of poetry and drama.[15] The term *rasa* primarily means "taste," "flavor," or "relish," but metaphorically it refers to the emotional experience of beauty in poetry and drama.[16] Bharata emphasized the inner aspect of the aesthetic experience — *rasa* as the essence of poetry or drama. Bharata does not really offer a technical analysis as to just how the aesthetic experience of *rasa* comes about. His explanation is in terms of a simple analogy. Just as a beverage results from the combination of various seasoned herbs, so the permanent mood of a drama, reinforced by various external representations such as words, gestures, and emotions *(bhāvas)*, produces a special aesthetic experience, or *rasa*.[17] In Bharata's view it is the *sthāyibhāva*, or the principal inner mood of the composition (e.g., love, grief, anger, or fear), that produces the *rasa*, or aesthetic experience. Such an inner mood runs through all other moods evoked like the thread of a necklace, and cannot be overcome by other opposed moods but only reinforced.[18] After this emphasis by Bharata on the inner aspect of aesthetic experience, the pendulum swung in the opposite direction and the essence of poetry was identified with its external aspects — its figures of speech *(alaṁkāras)* and poetic style *(rīti)*.[19]

In his *Dhvanyāloka*, however, Anadavardhana was able to subsume all of the pendulum swings of previous aesthetic theorizing. This he accomplished by basing himself on the *sphoṭa* model of Bhartṛhari and developing the notion of *dhvani* so that it referred not only to the evocative function of the uttered sounds (*alaṁkāra* and *rīti*) but also to inner mood/idea (*rasa*). In this way Anandavardhana established *dhvani* as the central notion of Indian aesthetics, and provided a definition for poetics that would include all rhythmic expression. Thus his *dhvani* theory presents itself as a development of the definition given by the first Indian poet Vālmīki — that rhythmic expression which is the spontaneous outlet of the mind overpowered by the grief caused by the death of one of the pair of *krauñca* birds would alone constitute poetry.[20] Anandavardhana not only included all rhythmic expression in his definition but also showed *dhvani* to be a key characteristic of such aesthetic experience.

After Anandavardhana, the next important *dhvani* literary critic is the great philosopher and poet of Kashmir, Abhinavagupta. Abhinavagupta lived ca. A.D. 1000. His two works on aesthetics are the *Locana*, a commentary on the *Dhvanyāloka*, and the *Abhinavabharatī*, a commentary on the *Nāṭya-śāstra*. Of these two it is the *Locana*, based upon Anandavardhana's *dhvani* theory, that Abhinavagupta himself judges to be most important. Of the two aspects of *dhvani* developed in the *Dhvanyāloka* — outer *dhvani* as the suggestive function of the uttered words, and inner *dhvani* as the suggested aesthetic mood itself — Abhinavagupta pays more attention to the latter. His interest here is both philosophical and religious. Whereas Anandavardhana seems to have paid equal attention to the inner and outer aspects of *dhvani* (although with an evident preference toward the inner), Abhinavagupta shifts the emphasis almost completely to the inner *dhvani*, which he calls the *ātman*, or soul, of the aesthetic experience.[21]

This development takes to its logical conclusion the direction that was already evident in the *Dhvanyāloka* and allows Abhinavagupta to make several theoretical moves in rapid order. In one stroke he overcomes rivalries between the *rasa* school and the *dhvani* school since they both now champion the same goal — that is, the inner essence of the aesthetic experience, which Abhinavagupta calls *rasadhvani*. In terms of philosophical analysis, the essence of poetry and drama is no longer located at the level of phenomenal experience (i.e., the external *dhvanis* of spoken words and heard sounds). Through aesthetics one is now seen to rise above the level of the individual enjoyment to the universal experience.[22] The uttered words and the meanings (*arthas*) they manifest are the mere particularities, like the outer adornments of the body. The true inner soul (which in Eastern thought is often conceived of as common to all men) of the aesthetic experience is the *rasadhvani* that the words and ideas evoke. Being beyond individual words and cognitions, *rasadhvani* is, according to Abhinavagupta, transcendental. There is intuitive union with ultimate reality. In the aesthetic experience one is completely caught up. Subject-object duality is overcome and there is a oneness with the universal *rasadhvani* itself. Pandey summarizes Abhinavagupta's final position as follows: "He holds that aesthetic experience at its highest level is the experience of the Self [Divine] itself, as pure and unmixed bliss."[23] It is the pure bliss of this highest universal *rasadhvani* that phenomenalizes itself into the various *rasas* and *dhvanis* of our aesthetic experience.

Although this is not the place to enter into a long discussion of the various categorizations in terms of numbers of *rasas*, it is perhaps interesting to note that Anandavardhana added the unorthodox *śānta* (spiritual serenity) to the orthodox list of eight *rasas*. In line with his universalizing and spiritualizing tendency, Abhinavagupta not only includes *śānta* but makes it the storehouse *rasa* for all others. In his view all *rasas* proceed from *śānta* and subside into *śānta*. *Śānta* is therefore not merely one of the *rasas*, but the vitalizing energy of all the other *rasas*.[24] *Śānta* therefore is the nature of the absolute *rasadhvani*, and gives *mokṣa* (spiritual self-realization) when one identifies with it fully. This seems to clearly reflect the absolutistic metaphysics present in Bhartṛhari's notion of *Śabdabrahman*.

III *A Criticism of the* Dhvani *Theory of Aesthetic Experience*

Perhaps the most potent criticism against the *rasadhvani* analysis of aesthetic experience is offered from the *anumāna*, or inference, school of Indian thought. Saṅkuka, an early commentator on Bharata's *rasa* theory, argues that *rasa* is not produced as an effect but inferred. What happens is that by the actor's clever portrayal of various gestures and words, the spectator is led to infer a mood within the actor that in fact does not exist. From this viewpoint, therefore, the aesthetic experience of *rasa* is nothing other than an illusion produced by a process of logical inference.[25]

Mahimabhaṭṭa, a younger contemporary of Abhinavagupta, offers a similar criticism against *dhvani* theory. In his *Vyaktiviveka* he attempts to show that *dhvani* is simply a variety of inference and therefore not different from ordinary word use. It is the unexpressed conclusion that the learned person reaches on hearing the poem that gives rise to aesthetic pleasure. The learned person is simply filling in the inferential steps that the poet has left out, and often this "filling-in" inferential activity will go on subconsciously so that the reader or spectator is not aware of it — suddenly the conclusion appears as if from nowhere, and one experiences *dhvani* or elation. Thus, in Mahimabhaṭṭa's eyes, *dhvani* is not a special aesthetic function in itself but is reduced to simply unconscious inference.[26] In this Mahimabhaṭṭa strongly attacks the *sphoṭa* theory of Bhartṛhari and the *dhvani* theory of Abhinavagupta in that both claim to transcend dualistic (subject-object) cognition in the inner realization — *sphoṭa pratibhā* for Bhartṛhari, and the transcendental *rasadhvani* for Abhinavagupta. Of course, if these are really only cases of unconscious reasoning (which as reasoning is necessarily dualistic) as Mahimabhaṭṭa contends, then *sphoṭa pratibhā* and *rasadhvani* are merely fictitious. Since Mahimabhaṭṭa's criticism rests on assumptions as to what happens within the unconscious during the aesthetic experience, a psychological analysis is required to see if he or *sphoṭa*/*dhvani* theory is supported.

IV *Psychological Processes in the Aesthetic Experience of* Dhvani

Although a psychological analysis of aesthetic experience should include at least some contemporary thinking, it is with the traditional Yoga psychology assumed by Bhartṛhari, Anandavardhana, and Abhinavagupta, that one must rightly begin. The ancient Yoga scholars arrived at their psychological description by subjectively analyzing thought processes. In our experience of a thought, a particular idea (*artha*) seems to arise, momentarily appear as self-illuminated before our mind's eye, and then pass away. Movement (*rajas*) therefore was conceived as a principal element of thought. Apart from *rajas*, thought, when its sensuous contents are removed, seems to exhibit a sort of universal form or mold. This *a priori* form appears to assume the structure of all contents presented to it. This is the universal knowing aspect of consciousness (*sattva*), which provides the substratum upon which the idea-particulars impose themselves for understanding. In the Yoga view the contents of thought are simply limitations of this universal aspect of *sattva*. *Tamas* is the material aspect of consciousness (i.e., the neural tissue of the brain) that becomes infused with energy and at the same time conserves energy, preventing its dissipation and providing for potentiality. In Yoga theory, *sattva*, *rajas*, and *tamas*, like three strands of a single rope, compose *all* the stuff of consciousness (*citta*).

Consequently, if it were possible to suddenly stop one's mental processes and take a cross section through one's psyche, it would reveal a quantitative relationship among *sattva*, *rajas*, and *tamas* that would be in keeping with the qualitative nature of the experience of that particular moment. For example, if it was a moment of clear intelligence *sattva* would be predominant and the other two aspects (*rajas* and *tamas*) would be proportionately reduced. A moment of pure passion would see *rajas* as predominant. An experience characterized as dullness or inertia would mean that one's *citta* was dominated by *tamas*. The infinite variety of relative weightings among the three aspects of *citta* correspond to the seemingly infinite variety of our mental states. Such states (*citta-vṛttis*) include all the possible modifications of *citta* that may be experienced in one's phenomenal existence. The Yoga analysis maintains that we cannot distinguish these states of consciousness from consciousness itself, for consciousness is not something separate from its states. Consciousness exists in its states. Thus, as Bhartṛhari states, thought or language and consciousness are one and the same.

Another basic finding of the Yoga analysis is that this unity of language and consciousness is identified with the Divine (*Īśvara* — consciousness as the universal forms of pure *sattva*) and is constantly seeking to burst forth into expression at the phenomenal level of thoughts and words. In Bhartṛhari's language theory these seed or *a priori* forms of word-consciousness are the universal *sphoṭas*, which manifest themselves through *rajas* and *tamas* as inner meanings (*arthas*) and uttered words and phrases (*dhvanis*). Such a primordial noumenal *sphoṭa* is psychologically analyzed as a pure concentrated intuition (*prajñā*), which is unitary in nature. Only as it becomes bifurcated into thought, as the first step toward uttered speech, does the subject-object duality of our ordinary cognition appear.

Perhaps it would be helpful to illustrate the above-discussed Yoga description with an introspective examination of our own experience in the act of speaking. At its earliest genesis the speaking act would seem to involve some kind of mental effort to tune out distracting sensations and thoughts, and inwardly focused concentration of mind, and an effort of the mind to bring into self-awareness some idea (or glimpse of reality) that is only vaguely within our ken. Although we may feel very sure of its presence just beyond the fringes of our conscious awareness, and although we may find ourselves impelled by a great desire to reveal that idea to ourselves in discursive thought, a great effort at concentrated thinking is often required before any clear conceptualization of it is achieved. Even then we may well feel dissatisfied in that the laboriously conceived conceptualization proves to be so inadequate and incomplete in comparison with our direct intuition of the noumenal "thing-in-itself," which remains stubbornly transcendent in the face of all our attempts to capture it in discrete thought. In Bhartṛhari's terminology, the noumenal idea or intuition would be the *sphoṭa*, the conceptualized inner meaning would be *artha*, and the spoken expression of that conceptualization would be *dhvani*.

The above introspection into the speaking act is a helpful beginning point for illustrating the special claim made by the aesthetic theories of *dhvani*. The difficulty in conceptualizing the noumenal idea into the words and phrases of ordinary language was very evident. Although Bhartṛhari maintained that each uttered word or *dhvani* manifested the whole of the *sphoṭa*, it did so only vaguely so that the full, or *prajña*, intuition was not accomplished on the first try. Subsequent words and phrases of the sentence would each again attempt to reveal the whole *sphoṭa*, and each would remove a little more of the vagueness until finally with the cognition of the last word (taken together in consciousness with the memory traces, or *saṁskāras*, of all the preceding words), the last obstructing vagueness would be removed and the *pratibhā*, or unitary intuition, of the *sphoṭā* spontaneously occur.[27]

The language critics seem to be suggesting that ordinary speaking, as analyzed by Bhartṛhari, does not have the power to fully reveal or make possible intuitive union with the *sphoṭa*. The ordinary *dhvanis* may well, by the psychological mechanism of *saṁskāras*, evoke inner meanings (*arthas*), but this will still be at the discursive level of subject-object cognition — the point at which philosophic inquiry inevitably seems to have to terminate. But this is unsatisfactory because it leaves one in the impotent situation of having vaguely glimpsed the truth "academically," as we say, yet been unable "to make it one's own." It is precisely at this juncture that the aestheticians see themselves as offering a helping hand to the philosopher or the theologian who has become entrapped in the limitations inherent in his own rational processes.

This helping hand comes in the aesthetic evocation of the underlying emotion (*rasadhvani*) in which the *artha* in its *a priori* form is embedded. Emotion is needed for the overcoming of dualistic cognition so that the unitary intuition of the *sphoṭa* can occur. Since the dualistic nature of ordinary language or rationality and inference can only vaguely suggest the *sphoṭa*, it is only by the *vyañjanā*, or suggestive power, of poetic and dramatic words and its resultant emotion (*rasadhvani*) that one can identify with the nondualistic intuition of the poet and so escape from the duality inherent in one's own ordinary cognition. This is the special power and function the aestheticians claim for their use of language. Perhaps the contemporary poet A. E. Housman put it well when he said, "And I think that to transfuse emotion — not to transmit thought but to set up in the reader's sense a vibration corresponding to what was felt by the writer — is the peculiar function of poetry."[28] The "vibration," or *rasadhvani*, is potentially present in all consciousness. The poet or dramatist does not create it as a new thing; he simply discovers what is already present through the excellence of his own intuition. His contribution is the skillful creation of a set of words and phrases that will awaken the spectator's sensitivity to that same intuition but this time in the spectator's consciousness. The beginning point for the poet and the ending point for the listener are the same universal intuition, or *rasadhvani*, which is inherent in all consciousness.

Abhinavagupta's description of the mental processes involved in the aesthetic experience is consistent with the above analysis. In his view each psyche has implanted within certain basic *sthāyibhāvas*, or dominant moods.[29] The *sthāyibhāvas* are the divinely given *saṁskāra* series of pure *sattva*, which, for Patañjali, compose Īśvara's pure forms. These pure *sattva* forms are the unmanifested *sthāyibhāvas*, and are but limitations within *sattva* of pure universal consciousness. This would be the Yoga description of the *rasa śānta* — the ground *rasadhvani* out of which the others arise. At this level of collective consciousness (*buddhitattva*), there is no subject-object distinction, and, as Vyāsa puts it, "all we can say is that it exists."[30] The poet or playwright first comes to know this universal *rasadhvani* as a unitary supersensuous perception (*pratibhā*). Since *sattva* is by definition pure bliss, and this is a "knowing by becoming one with *sattva*," the author's experience at this point is also bliss — but with a *rajas* impulse toward outer expression or manifestation. From this moment of highest inspiration flows forth his aesthetic creation, the rhythmic phrases and dramatic situations that evoke in the consciousness of the listener that same supersensuous perception the author experienced. The better the poet, the more effectively will his words (outer *dhvanis*) raise us away from the dullness (*tamas*) of our ordinary experience to an aesthetic climax (inner *dhvani*) that is pure and blissful (*sattvic*) in nature.

It is of considerable interest to note that an increasing number of contemporary psychologists are coming to support the ancient Indian contention that the mind contains its own structuring mechanism (*sphoṭas* or *rasadhvani*) without which aesthetic knowing would be impossible. For example, Karl Pribram, a neurophysiological psychologist, while studying memory found evidence suggesting that the brain contains structuring patterns within individual nerve cells that seem to resemble laser-produced holograms. When the appropriate sensory input patterns are presented, the latent hologram is aroused, resulting in the words and symbols that function as our means for knowing.[31] In Abhinavagupta's aesthetic theory, *rasadhvani* would be the functional equivalent of the nerve cells' hologram, and the outer *dhvanis* would correspond to the sensory input patterns.

Another point of contact between Pribram and *dhvani* theory is the former's emphasis upon inner feelings or dispositions as the motive power by which the external sensory patterns and the inner holograms are, as he puts it, grafted onto one another.[32] Following a similar line of theorizing, Wilder Penfield, a neurologist, likens the cerebral cortex to a carpet of nerve cells in which consciousness is recorded in a kind of permanent fashion.[33] Such "permanent" recordings (of past experiences) provide a *sphoṭa*-like model against which present experience is interpreted as meaningful. But, while there are many formal and functional similarities between the above-mentioned modern scientists and *dhvani* theory, it must be clearly understood that for modern Western thinkers inner mechanisms of consciousness (e.g., *sphoṭa* or *rasadhvani*) are usually taken as a learned expression of the external world, and not a beginningless inner entity that is related to both the individual's previous lives and the universal or collective consciousness of all beings.

Perhaps the only modern Western psychologist to maintain that all consciousness is collective and contains within itself in seed form the knowledge of reality is Carl Jung. In this regard Jung provides the closest modern Western approximation to the Yoga conception of consciousness. The psyche is defined by Jung as the totality of all conscious as well as unconscious mental processes.[34] For Jung, as is the case with Yoga, the stuff of consciousness is no less real than the physical matter of the external world.[35] The core constituents of consciousness are the archetypes that Jung defines as mankind's universal reactions to typical human situations of fear, hate, love, birth, death, the divine, and so on.[36] The Jungian archetypes bear some formal resemblance to the *sphoṭa* or *rasadhvani* in that it is described as a universal and eternal presence that represents the sum of the latent potentialities of the individual psyche.[37]

In agreement with Yoga psychology, Jung conceives of the archetype's external expression as occurring by a process of individuation. Jung calls the external expression a symbol, and it may take the form of a word, gesture, or, more often for Jung, a pictorial image. This expressed symbol would parallel the outer *dhvani*. Such external expressions (i.e., the poem, play, or painting) are never devised consciously but are gradually clarified as the pictorial or word motif moves from the level of the personal consciousness to the deeper level of the collective unconscious. There, says Jung, "the symbol becomes increasingly dominant, for it encloses an archetype, a nucleus of meaning that is not representable in itself but is charged with energy."[38] Jung's conception of the archetype as "not representable in itself" seems to correspond to the *rasadhvanis* as pure potentialities (*sattvic saṁskāra* series) in the universal consciousness (*buddhitattva*). The "nucleus of meaning" aspect of the archetype would relate to the *artha*, and the pictorial or word form to the outer *dhvani*. The energy charge of the archetype would be Jung's version of the emotion (*rasa*) required for the aesthetic unification or juxtaposition of all these aspects so that the unitary *rasadhvani* could be realized.

It is interesting to note that in describing this process of symbol formation Jung gives the "feeling" and "intuiting" functions of the psyche priority over "thinking" (logical inference) and "sensing." Emotion and intuition are the basic processes through which man must first make contact with his archetypes. Thinking and sensing (pure abstract philosophizing) on their own cannot firmly engage or evoke the archetype — although they are the necessary copartners of feeling and intuition once the latter have made contact with the archetype. Before meaningful external expression can take place (in the speaking act, for example), there must first be an inner intuition that reveals the meaning to be expressed. Both Yoga and Jung maintain that this is only achieved when the psyche, through emotion and intuition, gives priority to the eternal archetypes, *sphoṭas* or *rasadhvani*, which are universally present in consciousness. Herein, Jung notes, lies part of the difficulty for modern technological man. Because of the emphasis on "surface discursive thinking" and "empiric sensing" that our technology requires, there is a limited possibility for intuitive symbolization of the archetypes within consciousness — for the deeper aesthetic experiences (*rasadhvanis*).

Since all of the above psychological analysis seems to support *sphoṭa* and *rasadhvani* theory as against the inference theory of Śaṅkuka and Mahimabhaṭṭa, it would be worthwhile to take a moment to examine any psychological evidence in support of the inference interpretation. Although Patañjali's Yoga psychology indicates that the intuited experience of the whole is the ultimate nature of consciousness, and that *rasadhvani* is a true case of suggested or evoked intuition, there are a number of contemporary Western psychologists who, following Mahimabhaṭṭa, would argue for inference as consciousness's ultimate mode of knowing. C. R. Peterson and L. R. Beach attempt to argue that unconscious inferential reasoning is at the base of all man's so-called intuitive processes.[39] Their research is based on the assumption that man lives in an uncertain environment with which he must come to terms. It is theorized that people solve this situation by becoming intuitive statisticians and constantly making "intuitive good guesses." In this view, then, the aesthetic experience of a spectator would be nothing more than the result of his ability to quickly and subconsciously put together all the clues offered by the play or poem so that a unified mood would result. The evidence offered, however, is essentially in the realm of statistical problem solving. While this type of research may be able to *quantify* the technical problem-solving "intuition" of a scientist, logician, or mathematician in terms of unconscious inference, the aesthetic intuition seems to be a *qualitative* "something other than" the sum total of all the quantitative inferences. In the experience of art, music, and literature, it is the "being caught up in" a universal experience that seems to be the essence — as *sphoṭa/dhvani* theory maintains.

CHAPTER 5

Yoga in the Vairagya-Sataka *of Bhartrhari*

IN addition to establishing himself in the classical Indian tradition as a grammarian and a metaphysician, and having established a basis for literary criticism, Bhartṛhari is also well known for his Sanskrit poetry. In popular Indian thought Bhartṛhari is identified as a king who was discouraged by the inconstancy of women and was thus led to renounce the world of sensuous experience. One of his verses recounts the experience, with the depth and compactness that characterizes his poetry.

> She who is the constant object of my thought
> Is indifferent to me,
> Is desirous of another man,
> Who in his turn adores some other woman,
> But this woman takes delight in me . . .
> Damn her! Damn him! The God of love!
> The other woman! And Myself![1]

Tradition seems to have consistently maintained that Bhartṛhari, the poet, was the same Bhartṛhari who composed the *Vākyapadīya* and a commentary on the *Mahābhāṣya* of Patañjali. This ancient tradition identifying Bhartṛhari the poet with Bhartṛhari the grammarian was called into question by scholars writing around the turn of the century (e.g., M. R. Kale[2]), and more recently by D. D. Kosambi.[3] Kosambi's argument, however, although meticulously researched, depends for its strength on the Chinese pilgrim I-tsing's suggestion that the Bhartṛhari of the *Vākyapadīya* was a Buddhist. Since Bhartṛhari the poet shows no trace of Buddhism, Kosambi felt that there must be two different Bhartṛharis. However, as the previous discussion of the *Vākyapadīya* made clear, the contents of that work are thoroughly Brāhmanical in nature. This, plus the new dating of Bhartṛhari as prior to the fifth century A.D. (on the basis of

Bhartṛhari quotations in the works of Diṅnāga), has led recent scholarship to return much nearer the identity thesis of the classical tradition.[4] Not only does the author of this book adopt the traditional viewpoint on this question, but it is suggested that Bhartṛhari's assumption of Patañjali's classical Yoga in the *Vākyapadīya* (see Chapter 3) also occurs in his poetry and is further evidence for the identity thesis. Thus, in addition to introducing the reader to Bhartṛhari's poetry, this chapter takes as its point of focus the Yoga psychology assumed in the verses of the *Vairāgya-Śataka*.

I *Bhartṛhari the Poet*

Bhartṛhari's *Vairāgya-Śataka*, or "Hundred Verses on Renunciation," is a poem of ancient India that may still be found upon the lips of Indians today. The *Vairāgya* is the third in a trilogy of poems by Bhartṛhari, each one hundred verses in length. The other two poems are entitled the *Nīti-Śataka* (on politics and ethics), and the *Śriṅgāra-Śataka* (on passionate love). The fact that these very old poems are still a part of the consciousness of contemporary India is one important reason for their study. Perhaps even more important, however, is the way in which both the world-transcending ideals of Indian religion and the Indian experience of sensual love are held in tension within the poems. While the West has identified both full enjoyment of the senses and the rigorous renunciation of the senses with India, most often these two aspects have remained quite disconnected. Bhartṛhari's poetry, especially the *Vairāgya*, includes both the sensuous and the sense-renouncing aspects of the Indian consciousness in a way that presents a rounded exposure of India to the modern reader. In the *Vairāgya*, Bhartṛhari presents us with the creative tension between a profound attraction to sensual beauty and the yearning for liberation from it. From this study valuable insight may be gained as to how Indian religion, art, and culture can be at once so sensuous and so spiritual.[5]

A *śataka*, in Sanskrit poetry, is a hundred detached verses having a common theme such as *vairāgya*, or renunciation. Each four-line verse is intended to convey a complete mood, or *rasa*, and to stand on its own as an aesthetic entity. Bhartṛhari's verses are characterized by the amount of complex thought and detail that he compresses into a simple metrical pattern. Barbara Miller, who has successfully translated his verses into English, suggests that "the stanzas may be compared to the miniature paintings which illustrate the manuscripts of medieval India. Profusion is forced into a miniature mould; the mould is then expanded by exploiting the suggestive overtones (*dhvani*) of words and images."[6]

In India the life of an individual is divided into four different stages: the student stage, the householder stage, the withdrawal from worldly life into the forest, and finally the stage of the wandering hermit or holy man. Bhartṛhari's poems reflect one's spiritual development through these stages. The *Nīti-Śataka* comments on the life of worldly possessions and political power. The *Śriṅgāra-Śataka* sensitively evokes the erotic mood of love, which, along with the pursuit of worldly possessions and power, characterizes the householder stage of life. But even within this stage there are seeds of discontent that motivate the sensitive soul toward the withdrawal and spiritual discipline of the final two stages. Bhartṛhari's poetry captures this discontent in its revulsion against the sordidness of worldly life, and in its awareness that the delights of passionate love are at once beautiful and enslaving.

A man may tread the righteous path,
Be master of his senses,
Retire in timidity
Or cling to modest ways — only until
The seductive arrow-glances of amorous women
Fall on his heart,
Glances drawn to her ear,
Shot from the bow of her brow,
And winged by long black lashes.

The path which leads beyond
Your bounds, Saṁsāra,
Would be less treacherous
Were it not for intoxicating glances
Waylaying us at every turn. (*Śriṅgāra-Śataka*, *slokas* 35 and 43)

In the end it is through the renunciation described in the *Vairāgya-Śataka* that release from such worldly desires may be achieved. The *Vairāgya* presents a poetic picture of the renunciation of the last two stages of life. Here the ascetic finds the dispassionate tranquillity of the forest as he passes his days in meditation on the bank of a mountain river. Release from the worldly life of sense enslavement is accomplished through the discipline of Yoga, and this therefore is the dominant theme throughout the *Vairāgya-Śataka*.

Earlier in this book it was suggested that the Yoga psychology assumed by Bhartṛhari in his *Vākyapadīya* is the Yoga of Patañjali. Bhartṛhari's *Vairāgya* is also firmly based on that same Yoga, which begins with a diagnosis of the states of consciousness making up ordinary human experience (*kleśas*) and then details the eight steps to release (*yogāṇgas*).

II *Diagnosis of the Human Condition*

In his analysis of the states of consciousness (*citta vṛtti*) Patañjali finds that all ordinary experience may be divided into five types: ignorance (*avidyā*), eogism (*asmitā*), passion (*rāga*), disgust (*dveṣa*), and clinging to life (*abhiniveśa*).[7] On close examination, each of these is found to end in suffering; therefore they are classed as *kleśas*, or constantly changing painful states of consciousness. Patañjali's analysis brings out philosophical and psychological dimensions that parallel descriptions found in Bhartṛhari's poetry. The poetic parallels may well convey a more comprehensive understanding of the Yogic experience than the *sūtras* and commentaries alone can provide. It has long been the contention of Indian literary critics that the aesthetic consciousness (*rasadhvani*) evoked by poetry transcends the dry and partial descriptions of the scholars.

Avidyā is the beginningless ignorance that obscures the inherent omniscience of consciousness from view. Patañjali describes *avidyā* as the root *kleśa* of *citta*.[8] *Avidyā* is defined philosophically as the taking of the noneternal (*anitya*), the impure (*asuchi*), the painful (*duḥkha*), and the not-self (*anātman*) to be the eternal, the pure, the pleasurable, and the self.[9] Through the Yogic analysis, every kind of worldly experience, with its sensual attachment to objects, is in the end seen to give only temporary pleasure. Due to the insatiability of desire, sensual indulgence only results in a constant craving for more. Thus for the Yogin, every pleasure is seen as a pain in the making.

In the poetic vision of the *Vairāgya*, *avidyā* also appears as the root of suffering. In *sloka* 18, *avidyā* is depicted as an insect that stupidly jumps into the fire or a fish that through ignorance takes the baited hook.[10] The human being, however, with his power of intelligent discrimination should avoid the hook, but the power of ignorant passion is so deluding that he greedily eats the bait. Even the ravages of time cannot remove us from the grip of *avidyā*.

> My face is graven with wrinkles
> My head is marked with grey,

My limbs are withered and feeble —
My craving alone keeps its youth. (*sloka* 8)

Asmitā, or egoism, results from the taking of one's body and thoughts to be one's true self (*ātman*).[11] In *sloka* 70, Bhartṛhari captures the meaning intended by Patañjali.

You descend to nether worlds,
You traverse the sky,
You roam the horizon
With restless mobility my mind!
Why do you never, even in error,
Stumble on what is pure
And the true part of yourself,
That Brahman, through which
You would reach your final bliss?

It is from such deluded egoism that *rāga* springs forth. *Rāga*, says Patañjali, is a thirst for pleasure by one who has previously experienced pleasures (in this or previous lives) and remembers them.[12] The poet brings out the full fury of *rāga* by comparing the condition of an ignorant man with that of the enlightened Lord Śiva. "Ordinary persons when they give themselves up to enjoyment, lose all control and become slaves to them; so even when satiety comes they cannot detach themselves. But Śiva, who has [purged the ignorance from his mind], is unaffected by them."[13]

Dveṣa, or aversion, is the opposite of *rāga*. It also springs from the ego-sense, which having experienced and remembered pain feels anxiety for its removal.[14] For the sensitive poetic mind, such remembrance is indeed painful and urges one toward the Yogic path of release.

Abandon the depths of sensuous chaos,
That prison of torment!
The course reaching beyond toward bliss
Can instantly allay all pain.
Initiate then a peaceful mood!
Renounce your gamboling unsteady ways!
Forsake the ephemeral mundane passions!
Rest placid now, my thoughts! (*sloka* 63)

But such anxiety and aversion are often countered by the strong impulsion within ignorant egoism for its own survival. *Abhiniveśa*, shrinking from death and clinging to life, is found by Patañjali to be rooted in *avidyā* and to spring from egoism. It is an endless craving for one's self. In an image remarkably similar to Yeats's "An aged man is but a paltry thing, a tattered coat upon a stick,"[15] Bhartṛhari describes the body that "can raise itself but slowly on the staff" yet "still startles at the thought of dissolution by death."[16] Patañjali remarks that this fear of death is found in both the stupid and the wise and gives evidence that the round of birth and rebirth (*saṁsāra*) must have been experienced by all.[17]

Within the constant circle of *saṁsāra* both Patañjali and Bhartṛhari describe consciousness by analogy to the flow of a river. In the *Yoga Sūtras* the changing movement of mental states (*citta-vṛttis*) is said to be like a river whose flow is in two directions; toward good, and toward evil.[18] Within itself, pure *citta* has an inherent tendency to flow in the direction of good — and this can never be totally lost. But *citta* is polluted by the *karmic* seeds of past thoughts and actions, and these make consciousness flow in the opposite direction, creating the whirlpool of existence called *saṁsāra*. When one has dammed up the flow of *citta* toward objects seen (women, food, drink, power, etc.) by *vairāgya*, and opened the flood gates toward *mokṣa*, or release from *saṁsāra* by practice in discriminative knowledge, then *citta* will flow toward good.[19] In poetic terms the same complex situation is described by Bhartṛhari:

Hope is a river
Whose water is desire,
Whose waves are craving.
Passions are crocodiles,
Conjectures are birds
Destroying the tree of resolve.
Anxiety carves a deep ravine
And makes the whirlpool of delusion
Makes it difficult to ford.
Let ascetics who cross
To the opposite shore
Exult in their purified minds. (*sloka* 10)

Such is the diagnosis of man's ordinary mental state with its polluting *kleśas*. Now the question arises as to what treatment can be taken so that the pollution may be purged, the whirlpool stilled, and the peaceful purity of mind realized. The treatment offered by both Bhartṛhari and Patañjali is the renunciation of worldly desires by the concentration of *citta* through Yoga.

III *Treatment of the Human Condition*

Patañjali states that the practice of the *yogāṇgas*, or steps to Yoga, results in the purging of *karmic* impurities from the stream of consciousness so that its inherent omniscience may shine forth. The purifying action of the *yogāṇgas* is likened to an ax splitting off the offending *kleśas* from *citta.*[20] The *yogāṇgas* are listed by Patañjali as follows: *yama*, or restraints; *niyama*, or positive practices; *āsanas*, or Yogic postures; *prāṇāyāma*, or regulation of respiration; *pratyāhāra*, or freedom of the mind from domination by sensual objects; *dhāraṇā*, or concentration; *dhyāna*; or Yogic meditation; and *samādhi*, or trance.[21]

The first step on the path of Yogic treatment is *yama.* Patañjali lists five *yamas*, or self-disciplines, which when practiced will remove the gross *karmic* impurities from our ordinary mental state. *Ahimṣā*, or noninjury, is the root *yama* and requires nonviolence in thought as well as action.[22] The test for having mastered *ahimṣā* is that the peacefulness of one's *citta* will affect all other persons and animals within one's presence. The lion and lamb will lie down together beside the Yogin.[23] Or as Bhartṛhari puts it, "Blessed are those who live in mountain caves, meditating on Brahman, the Supreme Light, while birds devoid of fear perch on their laps and drink the tear drops of bliss that they shed in meditation."[24] Other than *ahimṣā*, the *yamas* include the practices of *satya*, or truthfulness; *asteya*, or nonstealing; *brahmacarya*, or control of sexual desire; and *aparigraha*, or the absence of avarice. These are effectively captured in a verse from the *Nīti-Śataka*, *sloka* 3:

> Refrain from taking life,
> Never envy other men's wealth,
> Speak words of truth,
> Give timely alms within your means . . .
> Dam the torrent of your craving,
> Do reverence before the venerable,
> And bear compassion for all creatures . . .

Together with the above restraints, the Yogin must observe a series of *niyamas*, or positive practices of body and mind. *Samtoṣa* is described by Patañjali as the absence of desire for more than the necessities of life.[25] It is sensitively captured in Bhartṛhari's poetry.

I dwell content in the hermit's dress of bark,
While you luxuriate in silken splendor.
Still, my contentment is equal to yours;
Disparity's guise is deceiving.
Now let him be called a pauper
Who bears insatiable greed;
But when a mind rests content,
What can it mean to be "wealthy" or "poor"? (*sloka* 53)

Tapas, or the practice of austerities, consists in bearing with equanimity the pairs of opposites such as heat and cold, hunger and thirst.[26] The poet concurs: "Nothing is good for the wise in this world excepting the practice of austerities!"[27] For Patañjali, *Īśvarapranidhana* is the offering up of all actions to the Lord, so that all work is done not for one's own self but for God.[28] For Bhartṛhari, the vision of the unrelenting approach of death leads him to take refuge in the Lord alone.[29] *Svādhyāya*, or the study of Vedic texts and the repetition of syllables (e.g., AUM) that lead to release, is revered by Patañjali[30] and Bhartṛhari. The poet maintains that while other vows may lead to worldly prosperity, the repetition of Vedic vows results in spiritual peace.[31]

In *sūtras* II:33 and 34, Patañjali states a most important psychological insight (today called "behavior therapy"), which seems to be a basic assumption for the practice of Yoga in all Indian systems. When a yogin while performing his *yogāṇgas* finds himself beset by doubts or desires, he should counteract such perverse thoughts (*vitarkas*) by the cultivation of their opposites (*pratipaksa bhāvanā*). Bhartṛhari not only captures this insight, but at the same time seems to identify this difficulty as being a particular weakness of the poet.

Her breasts, those fleshy protuberances,
Are compared to golden bowls;
Her face, a vile receptacle of phlegm,
Is likened to the moon;
Her thighs, dank with urine, are said
To rival the elephant's trunk.
Mark how this despicable form
Is flourished by the poets. (*sloka* 16)

Of course this kind of "cultivating of opposites" can be practiced on the male body with equal success if the Yogin happens to be a woman. Underlying this practical psychology is the theoretical analysis of how actualized *karmas* create a potency or *saṁskāra* for the repetition of the same act or thought to be laid down in the subconscious *citta* where the appropriate moment for a new actualization of the *karma* is awaited. Such habitual behavior or thought patterns are self-reinforcing in nature and can be broken only by the self-conscious act of creating sufficient opposing *karmas* so that even the unactualized *saṁskāras* will be rendered impotent.[32]

Āsansas, or body postures, are prescribed by Patañjali to control the restless activity of one's body — a necessary prerequisite to the controlling of one's mind. The *sūtra* describes the kind of posture required as being stable, motionless, and easy to maintain.[33] With all possible body movements restrained, the *citta* is left free for its efforts toward concentration. Toward the end of the *Vairāgya-Śataka* we find the poet adopting an *āsana*: "Sitting in peaceful posture, during the nights when all sounds are stilled into silence . . . fearful of the miseries of birth and death, crying aloud 'Śiva, Śiva, Śiva . . . .' "[34] Along with the practice of stable sitting the Yogin has to master controlled breathing, or *prāṇāyāma*. Although this practice is not specifically mentioned in the poem, it is clearly assumed in the repeated urgings toward a quiet and calm mind.[35] Regulation of breathing is based on the principle that there is a direct connection between the rate of respiration and mental states. This is known to the modern neurophysiologist and is easily observable by any layman. In states of emotional arousal (especially of the passionate variety so clearly examined in Bhartṛ*hari's Śriñgāra-Śataka*) respiration is uneven and fast, while in one who is concentrating it becomes rhythmical and slow. In such concentration there is also *pratyāhāra*, or withdrawal of the senses from attachment to external objects, and instead the inward focusing of the sense organs and all of *citta* on the *ātman*, or true self. As Bhartṛhari puts it, "Desist, O heart, from the troublous labyrinth of sense-objects; take that path of (highest) good which is capable of bringing about in a moment the destruction of endless troubles; get thee to the state of thy *Ātman*"[36]

The last three *yogāṇgas* (*dhāraṇā*, or fixed concentration; *dhyāna*, or Yogic meditation; and *samādhi*, or trance concentration) are not easily separated. Patañjali says that they represent three stages of the same process in which the subject-object duality of ordinary cognition is gradually purified until "oneness with the object" (knowing by becoming one with) is achieved.[37] As Vyāsa puts it, when fixed concentration shines forth only in the form of the object being contemplated and empty of all duality, that is *samādhi*.[38] In this state there is no self-awareness but only direct intuition — *citta*, or consciousness, knows by fusing itself with the object. And for both the

Yoga Sūtras and the *Vairāgya-Śataka*, the intended object is Brahman manifested as Lord (Īśvara for Patañjali; Śiva for Bhartṛhari).

> Purge your delusion
> Find joy in moon-crested Śiva,
> Dwell in devotion, my thoughts,
> On the banks of the heavenly river! . . . (*sloka* 64)

Through intense devotional concentration on Brahman as the Lord, a final stage of transcendent consciousness is reached. At this rarefied height words are quite inadequate. Patañjali technically terms the experience *nirvicāra samādhi*. It is the state achieved when by constant practice the mind loses the notions of time, place, and causality, and becomes one with the essence of its object of concentration, namely; Brahman.[39] Bhartṛhari, through the poetic form, perhaps comes close to expressing this experience:

> O Earth, my mother! O Wind, my father! O Fire, my friend! O Water, my good relative! O Sky, my brother! here is my last salutation to you with clasped hands! Having cast away Infatuation with its wonderful power, by means of an amplitude of pure knowledge resplendent with merits developed through my association with you all, I now merge in the Supreme Brahman. (*sloka* 100)

CHAPTER 6

The Contribution of Bhartṛhari

I *Bhartṛhari's Contribution to India*

FOR several centuries before Bhartṛhari the people of India had been falling away from their traditional Brāhmanical roots. Jainism and Buddhism had flourished. The fact that these two heterodox schools accepted no revelation and treated language as merely conventional had the effect of calling the Vedas into question. The ancient scriptures were questioned in terms of their authority and their ability to effect release, or *mokṣa*. In addition there appears to have been a proliferation of shallow and sometimes superstitious image worship among the Hindus. Bhartṛhari, along with his predecessor Patañjali, may well have played a significant role in arresting this trend and recovering much of the essence of the Brāhmanical tradition. Throughout Bhartṛhari's grammar, metaphysics, and poetry, the Vedas regain their rightful place as the source of all knowledge. The spoken word is seen as filled with divine power and the Yoga of the Divine Word is shown to be a path to *mokṣa*.

In countering the attack of Jainism and Buddhism on the authority of the Veda as revelation, Bhartṛhari agreed with the Mīmāṁsā teachers that the Veda is eternal and impersonal. But whereas it is the Vedic letter-sounds that are the eternal meaning-bearing units of language for the Mīmāṃsā. Bhartṛhari formulates a new theory as to how words convey meaning. In Bhartṛhari's view it is the whole word, or *sphoṭa*, that is the eternal meaning-bearing unit of language. Bhartṛhari turned the logic of the Mīmāṁsā on its head. Whereas for the latter it is the sum of the given parts that produces the whole meaning, Bhartṛhari shows that it is logically necessary for the whole to be primary, producing the parts (i.e., sentences and words) as secondary manifestations. Otherwise, unitary meaning could not be experienced. Not only was the priority of the whole established by logic, but Bhartṛhari further maintained that this whole, or *sphoṭa,* could be verified through intuition or supersensuous perception *(pratibhā).* And the nature or composition of this perceived *sphoṭa* is nothing other than pure consciousness (Brahman) inextricably intertwined with pure meaning (Veda). Thus, for Bhartṛhari, ultimate reality is defined as *Śabdabrahman,* and, at its highest level, is directly experienced through supersensuous intuition. The Divine is known and experienced, not through philosophical inference or objectless meditation, but by becoming aware of the Divine Word — consciousness that is already present within the mind of each being. *Śabdabrahman* is one although manifested in many words, the Vedas. It is through the many words of the Vedas, spoken by the *ṛṣi* and latently present within all consciousness, that one may come to know and experience the unitary *Śabdabrahman* and obtain *mokṣa.*

The *sphoṭa* theory of Bhartṛhari's *Vākyapadīya* not only established language as divine and the Vedas as revelation, it also provided a firm foundation for the mysticism of the word. The chanting of AUM and other *mantras,* which has come to occupy such a central position in Indian religion, is placed on a firm foundation by Bhartṛhari. With his concept of *Śabdabrahman* Bhartṛhari provided fresh insight into the ancient Vedic revelation of *vāk,* or speech, as the essence of both consciousness and the divine. The *Ṛg Veda* puts it as follows:

> 3. I *[Vāk]* am the queen, the gatherer-up of treasures, most thoughtful, first of those who merit worship.
> Thus Gods have stablished me in many places with many homes to enter and abide in.
> 4. Through me alone all eat the food that feeds them, — each man sees, breathes, hears the word outspoken.
> They know it not, but yet they dwell beside me. Hear, one and all, the truth as I declare it.
> 5. I, verily, myself announce and utter the word that gods and men alike shall welcome. I make the man I love exceeding mighty, make him a sage, ṛṣi, and a brāhmin.[1]

The repetition of *vāk* in the form of suitable sacred syllables, chosen by the *guru* to suit the spiritual level of the student's consciousness, evokes *Śabdabrahman* and simultaneously dispels the obscuring ignorance of impure language usage in previous lives. Chanting of the *mantra* had this effect, because, as Bhartṛhari shows, it is nothing other than a clear and powerfully evocative manifestation of the

Divine Word–consciousness *(Śabdabrahman).* Bhartṛhari's contribution was to provide India with a defensible metaphysical explanation of this time-honored belief in the power of chanting *mantras.* And when Bhartṛhari's explanation is examined in the light of Patañjali's *Yoga Sūtras,* an understanding of the detailed psychological processes involved is also achieved.

In technical or scholastic Indian philosophy Bhartṛhari's *sphoṭa* theory is of definite interest in the way that it contrasts with Śaṅkara's analysis as to the process by which error is overcome. Both Bhartṛhari's philosophy of language and Śaṅkara's Advaita Vedānta are absolutistic monisms in which error *(avidyā)* plays the important role of obstructing the real from view. Whereas Śaṅkara describes the error as being transcended via a single negation (e.g., as when it is realized "this is not snake"), Bhartṛhari holds that error (e.g., the vagueness of the perception of the whole in its first presentation — as when the first letters of a word are uttered) is positively overcome by the increasingly clear cognition of the whole *(sphoṭa),* which the succeeding perceptions reveal. For Śaṅkara there is only true or false cognition, and error is overcome by a single negation of the false, which simultaneously completely reveals the real. Bhartṛhari, by contrast, analyzes the overcoming of error as a progressive approximation to the real. While the first perception may be quite vague, the second will be less so, the third will be increasingly clear, until finally with the final perception all vagueness or error is overcome by the positive perception of the real in its wholeness. For Śaṅkara the process is a single all or nothing inferential negation; for Bhartṛhari it is a series of perceptions with an increasingly positive approximation to the real.

In Śaṅkara's theory, the realization of *mokṣa* would be a sudden realization experience requiring a radical change in the way the universe is experienced. One's experience would suddenly "flipover" from *maya,* or worldly illusion, to Brahman as the ground or essence of all. This would approximate what William James has called "the sick-soul conversion experience."[2] For Bhartṛhari, the realization of *mokṣa* would likely be the result of a gradual change. The *karma* of the obscuring *avidyā* is continuously "burnt up" through Yogic meditation and chant. The removal of error through gradual purifying of *vāk,* or speech, results in the spiritual realization of *mokṣa.* Bhartṛhari's view does ring true to human experience and seems very close to William James's category of "healthy-minded" religious experience.[3]

In addition to explaining how error may be overcome, all absolutistic Indian philosophy has had to grapple with the problem of how error comes to be in the first place. How is it that the one Brahman, absolute in his perfection, comes to be manifested as the imperfect world of ordinary experience? The Hindu scriptures suggest various answers. The *Bṛihadāranyaka Upaniṣad* quotes the *Ṛg Veda* as saying that Indra can cause himself to appear in many forms through the magic power of *māyā*.[4] The *Śvetāśvatara Upaniṣad*, in the course of discussing the one God of the manifold world, describes *māyā* as the illusion of a manifold world projected by the *māyin*, or illusion maker, out of Brahman.[5] In the *Bhagavad-Gītā*, *māyā* is expressed as the Lord's divine power, consisting of the three qualities of nature *(guṇas)* that delude men.[6]

Bhartṛhari makes a genuine contribution to this discussion by suggesting that *Śabdabrahman* or Word-consciousness itself contains an inner energy *(kratu)* that seeks to burst forth *(sphut)* into expression. In Bhartṛhari's theory it is because of the "inner energy" of the meaning-whole, or *sphoṭa*, that this unity comes to be expressed in the diversity commonly called speech. What appears to be unitary is seen to contain all the potentialities of multiplicities and complexities of the manifested world. The *Vākyapadīya* maintains that, in addition to this pent-up potentiality for bursting forth, the inner energy of speech contains another aspect — the desire to communicate. For Bhartṛhari it is through this desire to communicate that *Śabdabrahman* expresses grace and compassion by revealing himself. From the viewpoint of individual beings, it is this same desire to communicate that causes the young child to utter his first words. Learning to speak is simply the process of the Word-consciousness being transformed through its own inner energy into the manifested language of the particular community into which the child was born. This discussion of the notion of the inner energy, or *kratu*, of *Śabdabrahman* illustrates the greatness of Bhartṛhari for Indian thought. Here is a conception that is basic for solution of the metaphysical problem of how the absolute becomes manifested as the many, and yet at the same time provides a linguistic theory for the genesis and development of language in the young child.

Bhartṛhari's metaphysical solution of the problem of how the absolute becomes many compares favorably with the more widely known explanation of Śaṅkara. According to Śaṅkara, Brahman, or the absolute, is the necessary cause that potentially contains and projects the manifold world (the effect) and yet is in no way exhausted by this production.[7] Only on the basis of this understanding of cause and effect, says Śaṅkara, is it possible to uphold that by the knowledge of the one reality, the knowledge of all else is attained. Similarly, on this theory of cause and effect, the one-sided identity relationship between the ground and its appearances, between Brahman and *māyā*, is made clear. Here Śaṅkara conceives of *māyā* as a limiting condition *(upādhi)* of Brahman in a way that bears marked similarity to Bhartṛhari's conception of time *(kāla)* as a limiting function of *Śabdabrahman*. Although it is usually suggested that Śaṅkara, following his teacher Gauḍapāda, formulated this conception of *māyā* by borrowing from the absolutistic logic of Mādhyamika and Yogācāra Buddhism, it seems quite feasible to suggest that he may also have learned from Bhartṛhari's absolutism. Bhartṛhari, after all, did live several centuries before Śaṅkara, and the *Vākyapadīya* was widely known then as now. In fact there is good evidence for suggesting that Śaṅkara knew Bhartṛhari's work, for he takes great pains in attempting to refute *sphoṭa* as the meaning-bearing unit of language.[8] In any case, it is quite clear that both thinkers employ the notion of some kind of limiting condition *(upādhi)* as the mechanism by which the absolute manifests itself as many. Bhartṛhari used it earlier and may have suggested its usage to Śaṅkara.

A difficulty encountered in Śaṅkara's thinking is that he argues for the impersonality and eternality of the Veda, while at the same time suggesting that God is somehow the eternal omniscient author. Making reference to the *Chandogya Upaniṣad* (4.15.1), Śaṅkara argues that the Veda itself states that it is but breath of the Divine. As easily as one breathes out, so God produced the Veda — as if in cosmic play. Due to its self-evident omniscience and omnipotence, nothing but Brahman can be inferred as its cause.[9] In his philosophical argument Śaṅkara distinguishes between "evolution of the world from Brahman" and "evolution of the world from *śabda* or Veda." Brahman, he maintains, is the material cause of the world while *śabda* is only an efficient cause.[10] As to what is the originating will that lies behind the operation of *śabda* as efficient cause, Śaṅkara says only that it is the mysterious desire of Brahman to get into diversity from unity.[11] Bhartṛhari's philosophy seems more convincing on this issue. *Śabdabrahman*, as the intertwined unity of word and consciousness, is at once both the material and efficient cause of the Veda and the world. And for Bhartṛhari no mysterious will of Brahman needs to be postulated to explain the manifestation of the absolute. It is the inherent *kratu*, or bursting forth of the *sphoṭa* into expression, that is the very nature of the Divine Word—consciousness.

In evaluating the above-mentioned arguments of Śaṅkara and Bhartṛhari, it is interesting to note that one of Śaṅkara's favored disciples interprets his master's teaching so that it approximates the position of Bhartṛhari. Tradition has it that out of his immediate followers, Śaṅkara chose Padmapāda as the one to compose a commentary on his *bhāṣya;* thus the *Pancapādikā* was written.[12] In it Padmapāda argues that a primal *avidyā,* which is beginninglessly existent in Brahman, is the cause of *māyā,* or error. From its existence in Brahman, *avidyā* through its projective power manifests absolute Brahman as the Vedas and the world. Thus, for Padmāpada, Veda (as *avidyā),* in its beginningless coexistence with Brahman, is the material *and* efficient cause of the phenomenal world.[13]

This is the same kind of explanation Bhartṛhari had provided in his *Vākyapadīya* several centuries earlier. In it there is the recognition that God, as absolute, must be the source and cause of all manifestation. From the viewpoint of an individual being, the limited manifestation he perceives (e.g., the portion of the Vedas he hears) is error because he takes it to be absolute. In philosophic terms, he mistakes some of the parts for the whole. But although the manifested parts occasion the error they simultaneously provide for its correction. Padmapāda agrees with Bhartṛhari's theory that it is through the parts (e.g., the words and sentences of the various Vedas) that the whole (e.g., Brahman or *Śabdabrahma)* is known. *Māyā,* or error, is simultaneously helpful and hindering. The helpful *māyā* allows one to see through it to the absolute. The unhelpful function comes when the parts projected out of the whole hide the whole by attributing absolute reality to themselves. To the objection that locating the cause of error (the projecting of the parts) in the absolute (the whole) means that the absolute itself is error, Bhartṛhari and Padmapāda answer that while error is inherent in the absolute, it is nullified by the absolute's knowledge that that is its nature. Therefore, the absolute can use error as a power.[14] For Bhartṛhari, this is *Śabdabrahman* manifested as the Vedas; for Padamapāda and Śaṅkara, it is Brahman manifested as Īśvara.

Bhartṛhari's absolutistic metaphysics was also attacked and imitated by Buddhist scholars. The Buddhist Śāntaraksita, who lived after Bhartṛhari, attacks the notion of *Śabdabrahman* in his well-known work *The Tattvasaṅgraha.*[15] The attack on Bhartṛhari is as follows. If *Śabdabrahman* is absolute reality, how can its manifestation into the parts of the world that are not *śabda*, or word, be possible? How, for example, can word-consciousness account for the manifested experience of the color "blue?" Bhartṛhari's response would be that the Buddhist's very use of the word "blue" in his question is only possible because of the fact that the word-consciousness or *sphoṭa* "blue" is present and the basis for every "blue" experience. Only then could the letters *b, l, u, e* communicate meaning in direct experience or in uttered language.

The imitation of Bhartṛhari by the Buddhists comes when the Mahāyāna Yogācāra school accepts the philosophic approach of levels of truth.[16] In the *Vākyapadīya* Bhartṛhari provides for "outer" and "inner" levels of language and meaning. The "outer" or expressed levels of language (*vaikharī vāk*, or uttered speech, and *madhyamā vāk*, or thought) are distinguished from the "inner" intuition of the *paśyantī vāk*, which is the absolute word. The lower levels are simply projection by the absolute of itself. The Yogācāra Buddhists, who reach their height at about the same time as Bhartṛhari, also describe the absolute in terms of pure inner consciousness *(vijñāna)*. In Yogācāra theory the two "outer" or expressed levels of the inner consciousness are *ālaya-vijñāna* (the storehouse of all potential mental states) and *pravṛtti-vijñāna* (the gross level of empirical experience). The Yogācāra levels have a marked similarity to Bhartṛhari's levels, especially since in both cases it is the absolute inner consciousness that is projecting itself outward into the two lower levels. This similarity is especially interesting when it is noted that the Buddhist Diṅnāga, who was one of the main Yogācāra scholars, lived just after Bhartṛhari and quotes from the *Vākyapadīya*.[17]

Aside from this apparent influence on Buddhism, Bhartṛhari's formulation of levels of language has strongly influenced the Hindu Kashmir Pratyabhijñā school. This school fully adopted Bhartṛhari's conception of the absolute as an intertwining of word and consciousness that expresses itself through the levels of language. The change introduced by the Kashmir school is the use of *parā vāk* and *Parā Brahman* where Bhartṛhari would usually use *paśyantī vāk* and *Śabdabrahma*. While these changes do not significantly alter the logic or intent of the metaphysics established by Bhartṛhari, they do allow the Kashmir school to include Śiva within their metaphysical model, for religious purposes.[18]

Bhartṛhari's contributions to Indian aesthetics have been just as significant as his contributions to philosophy and metaphysics. He directly contributed to India's literature as a poet of the fifth century. The measure of the excellence of his verse is that, some fifteen centuries later, it evokes deep emotion when reverently spoken by present-day Hindus. His poetry has taken its place alongside the works of Kālidāsa and Daṇḍin in the Indian poetic consciousness. An indication of this high estimate is the fact that the modern-day saint and poet Sri Aurobindo has translated Bhartṛhari's verses from Sanskrit into English poetry.[19] It is evident that the spiritual insight of Bhartṛhari's poetry is especially revered by Aurobindo. Even the more recent secular poets writing in India today share Bhartṛhari's search for his true self, although their methods and approaches may be quite different. While the modern day materialistic *Playboy/Playgirl* culture may have replaced the sensuous opulence of the king's court, the entrapment of the senses and the meaninglessness of life that ensues is the same. Although the Yoga solution offered in the *Vairāgya* and the existentialism of the contemporary poet may seem far apart, the basic quest for self-realization is held in common.

In addition to his poetry, Bhartṛhari's language theory in the *Vākyapadīya* has been shown (in Chapter 4) to have provided Indian literary criticism with its notion of *dhvani*. Bhartṛhari's conception of *dhvani*, as the uttered word that evokes the inner *sphoṭa*, or meaning-whole, is given further development by the literary critic Anandavardhana. Anandavardhana specializes the notion of *dhvani* so that it refers to the specific aesthetic sense evoked, rather than the ordinary meaning. In the hands of the literary critics *dhvani* comes to mean the special suggestive function *(vyañjanā)* of the poetic phrases or dramatic events. But Anandavardhana also uses *dhvani* to refer to the total inner mood that is suggested. In terms of Bhartṛhari's language model, this usage would seem to parallel the notion *sphoṭa* as the meaning-whole manifested by the spoken words *(dhvanis)*. Anandhavardhana's development of *dhvani* so as to include both the suggestive function of the uttered verse and the inner mood *(rasa)* that is evoked, resulted in a theory of literary criticism that was able to unify and transcend many earlier theories (from Bharata's emphasis upon the principle inner mood, or *rasa*, to the opposite extreme of the identification of poetry with its external figures of speech and poetic style). In his *Dhvanyāloka*, Anandavardhana was able to subsume all the pendulum swings of previous aesthetic theorizing. This he accomplished by basing himself on the *sphoṭa* model of Bhartṛhari and developing the notion of *dhvani* so that it referred not only to the evocative function of the uttered sounds *alaṁkāra* and *rīti)* but also to the inner mood/idea *(rasa)* evoked.

Abhinavagupta, the great philosopher and poet of Kashmir, gives further development to the notion of *dhvani*, and, in so doing, returns nearer to Bhartṛhari's basic logic of the superiority of the inner over the outer, the whole over the parts. Of the two aspects of *dhvani* developed in the *Dhvanyāloka* — outer *dhvani* as the suggestive function of the uttered words, and inner *dhvani* as the aesthetic mood itself — Abhinavagupta focuses attention upon the latter, which he renames *rasadhvani*. The true inner soul of the aesthetic experience is the *rasadhvani* that the words and ideas evoke. Being beyond the individual words and cognitions, *rasadhvani* is transcendental. It is the pure bliss of the Divine that phenomenalizes itself into the various *rasas* and *dhvanis* of aesthetic experience. Thus, for Abhinavagupta, the highest universal *rasadhvani* (which he calls *śānta*, or spiritual serenity) leads to *mokṣa* when one identifies with it fully. This development within Indian literary criticism clearly reflects its dependence upon the absolutistic metaphysics of Bhartṛhari's *Śabdabrahman*.

Having recognized Bhartṛhari's contribution to the Indian schools of literary criticism, it is interesting to speculate on how Bhartṛhari (if he were alive today) might respond to the notion of *dhvani* as aesthetic suggestion. The literary critics' claim is that only via *vyañjanā*, or aesthetic suggestion, with its crucial emotional component, can the ultimate universal unity of consciousness be realized. This unity, it is held, could not be achieved via the ordinary manifesting power of words that is described by Bhartṛhari's *dhvani–artha–sphoṭa* analysis. In short, it suggests that Bhartṛhari's *sphoṭa pratibhā* would be somehow incomplete when compared with Abhinavagupta's *rasadhvani*. To this Bhartṛhari might well reply that an impartial look at *dhvani* in the *Vākyapadīya* indicates that it includes all aspects of the aesthetic expression — all gesture, accent, style, metaphor, et cetera, — so does it not also include this notion of aesthetic suggestion *(vyañjanā)*? Perhaps Bhartṛhari's *dhvani–artha– sphoṭa* is all that is needed to fully account for aesthetic experience. Since he was a poet as well as a philosopher, it would seem strange if his philosophy of language did not include and account for poetic experience.

Bhartṛhari's full importance to Indian thought is seen when one includes, in addition to all of the above-mentioned achievements, his contributions to Sanskrit grammar. He gives further clarification to problems such as the interpretation of complex compound sentence structures in Sanskrit. Bhartṛhari's contributions to Sanskrit grammar are a further development of the interpretation offered by Patañjali in his *Mahābhāṣya*. The particular contribution of Bhartṛhari was that in the *Vākyapadīya* he gathered up the insights of the ancient grammarians Pāṇini, Kātyāyana, and Patañjali into a unified system, or *darśana*, through the practice of which one could attain liberation. Of Bhartṛhari's contribution to Sanskrit grammar, K. A. S. Iyer says that to him must be given the credit for pulling together for the first time, the general and particular notions that form the basis for the Sanskrit language. The idea of *sphoṭa* that emerged from this systematization throws light, not only on the Sanskrit language, but on the nature of language in general.[20] However, it must be remembered that should any originality of thought be attributed to Bhartṛhari himself, he would refuse to accept it; for, as he repeatedly emphasizes, he is doing nothing more than drawing out the insights given in the Vedas themselves.

II *Bhartṛhari's Contribution to the Wider World*

While some influence from Bhartṛhari's thought was very early carried into Tibet and China by Buddhist pilgrim scholars returning home from Nālundā University, it is only during the last century that Bhartṛhari's thought has reached the West. Now that critical editions of his Sanskrit works are being carefully edited and printed along with translations such as those by K. A. S. Iyer, Bhartṛhari's thought is finally being opened to the Western world. It may be quite correct to suggest that today, some fifteen centuries after Bhartṛhari lived, his contribution to the wider world is just beginning to be made. The following discussion will provide an indication of the potential contribution of Bhartṛhari's writings to modern philosophy, psychology, aesthetics, and religion.

The question of how language conveys knowledge in ordinary interpersonal communication, or of how language reveals knowledge in intrapersonal reflection, has long attracted the attention of philosophers in both the East and the West. Speculation as to the relation between thoughts, words or sentences, and the reality to which they refer, has been one of the oldest preoccupations of the human mind. The contemporary Western philosopher W. M. Urban clearly expresses the relationship between language and knowledge: ". . . the problem of what we can know is so closely bound up with the question of what we can say, that all meditation on knowledge involves meditation on speech."[21] In considering modern philosophy, it is worth noting that a nineteenth- and early twentieth-century renewal of interest in language in the West was influenced by scholars such as von Humboldt,[22] Max Müller,[23] and Cassirer,[24] all of whom gave considerable attention to the Sanskrit grammarian tradition systematized by Bhartṛhari.

Ernst Cassirer develops a philosophy of symbolic forms that has much in common with Bhartṛhari. Just as Bhartṛhari takes the *sphoṭa* as basic, so Cassirer takes the symbol to be essential for human knowledge. Taking the symbolic form as the common factor in all human endeavors (language, art, religion, science, etc.) provides each one with a theoretical claim to its own knowledge as being valid, and it allows the disparateness of these endeavors to complete and complement one another — since all are within the same (symbolic) universe of discourse. And in its function of distinguishing the ideal from the actual, the symbolic form, in each sphere of human endeavor, serves to continually open up new horizons for development. While the logic is that of Bhartṛhari — that is, that the whole is greater than the parts (the symbolic universe is greater than the individual symbolic forms) — Cassirer is not so rigorous as Bhartṛhari. Cassirer refuses to allow all the various manifestations of symbolism in science, art, religion, and so on, to come from one common source. Nor does Cassirer allow for the symbolic ideal to be completely achieved, whereas for Bhartṛhari this is the end-goal, or *pratibhā* experience. Like Bhartṛhari, however, Cassirer attributes the arising of symbolic expression to "instinct," or *kratu,* as it is called in Sanskrit.

A major difference between modern philosophy and Bhartṛhari occurs with reference to the notion of levels of language and truth. Here Bhartṛhari's thought has much in common with the Greek philosophy of Plato, but is strongly challenged by modern linguistic analysis. Plato conceived of eternal word-forms, a notion very similar to Bhartṛhari's *sphoṭas.* Also for Plato, as the parable of the cave indicates, reality is conceived on two levels — the projected shadow-truth of ordinary experience, as contrasted with the intuited level of Divine Forms. However, although this two-level view of reality and language appears to have been present in the early roots of the Western tradition, it seems quite lacking in modern thought. Now "truth" is taken to be "factual" or "empirical" — which by definition excludes the metaphysical. From Bhartṛhari's viewpoint this is the cause of the modern Western anxiety when contemporary cataloguings of empirical facts appear bereft of any deeper unifying ground or absolute truth referent, and therefore seem to become totally relative and atomistic in themselves. Bhartṛhari's philosophy may provide a helpful corrective or challenge to this dilemma of modern man.

One contemporary philosopher who already seems to have turned in Bhartṛhari's direction is Noam Chomsky. Chomsky has recently suggested that within consciousness there are certain innate universal grammatical structures.[25] These structures function something like computer programs within consciousness and in some ways resemble Bhartṛhari's *sphoṭas*. However, a major difference is that whereas the inherent structures of consciousness seem to be neutral in terms of meaning content for Chomsky, the *sphoṭa* is conceived by Bhartṛhari as being the very essence of meaning. From Bhartṛhari the pertinent question for Chomsky would be, "How can you have a nonmeaningful or neutral structure when the very function of structuring or programming incoming stimuli necessarily assumes the preexistence of a meaning-whole — otherwise would not the structuring occur on a basis of pure chance?" As is the case with a computer program, the organizing program or structure must itself possess a meaning logic that enables the incoming data to be processed into a meaningful result.

Among modern Western psychologists there seems to be increasing recognition of the need for some kind of inner structuring mechanism such as Bhartṛhari's *sphoṭa*. Like Bhartṛhari, William James feels that in thinking, meaning arises basically from the whole idea or unified mental state and not from a summation of the parts or component sensations.[26] Chapter 4 mentioned the neuropsychologist Karl Pribram, who finds it necessary to argue for some kind of inner structuring mechanisms in consciousness itself. Starting at the other side, as it were, from the spoken or uttered word, the theorizing of the contemporary cognitive psychologists Heintz Werner and Bernard Kaplan seems to closely follow Bhartṛhari. They attempt to answer the question of how it is possible that a material sound pattern — so technically different in substance and qualities from the object of perception or thought that it can come to symbolize — can ever be exploited for the representation of such an object.[27] In formulating the problem thus, Werner and Kaplan seem to converse in terms virtually identical to Bhartṛhari's discussion of language: "material sound pattern" for *dhvani*, "object of perception or thought" for *artha*, and "symbol" for *sphoṭa*. In their theoretical and experimental studies Werner and Kaplan found that there is an inherent expressiveness residing in objects and in vocalization patterns. It is this inner expressiveness that, much like Bhartṛhari's desire to burst forth into expression *(kratu)*, enables word symbols to be meaningful. Of course, there are definite points of difference. The word-symbol is a human construction based on a phenomenal object for Werner and Kaplan. Bhartṛhari's *sphoṭa,* by contrast, is a divinely established unity of word and consciousness. It is precisely on this question, namely; the nature and origin of the word symbol, that Bhartṛhari's thinking can creatively challenge a modern view such as the theory of Werner and Kaplan.

A leading cognitive psychologist, Jean Piaget, has recently suggested that knowledge results from a process of assimilation of sensory stimuli from the lower specialized sensory organs to the higher functions of the nervous system in accordance with an autoregulatory cognitive model. This would seem to support the *sphoṭa* interpretation of hearing as an integrative process in which the phonemes are perceived as meaningful due to the cognitive structuring they are given by the *sphoṭa.* This parallel is further supported when Piaget notes that such an autoregulatory cognitive mechanism appears as a whole that is conserved throughout a series of transformations (in both the individuation and assimilation directions). Piaget, of course, rejects the *sphoṭa* claim that the knowledge model is innate, but admits the necessity for some kind of autoregulatory knowledge mechanism and recognizes the infinite regression that results when the *a priori* existence of such a mechanism (e.g., *sphoṭa*) is not admitted.[28]

This assumption of the whole as *a priori* is also accepted by O. H. Mowrer when he suggests that a human infant becomes able to say or hear a word by virtue of the fact that "he already 'knows' what it sounds like and can practice the response against the model which already exists (in memory or 'imagination')."[29] The neurophysiological analysis of speech and brain mechanisms by Wilder Penfield also concludes with an integrative model that is similar to the *sphoṭa* theory. Penfield finds that the speech mechanism consists of two integrated halves. There is a "sound unit," a "conceptual unit," and an integrative connection between the two.[30] As is the case with the *sphoṭa* analysis, Penfield finds that the conceptual unit seems to provide the neural integration for the speech unit. Penfield suggests that there is a "conceptual storehouse" of such integrative speech mechanisms existing in the brain, but cautions that neither the place of storing nor the manner of their activation is understood.[31]

Understanding of meaning occurs, he says, when the sound unit and the conceptual unit are established together with their interconnections. In Penfield's theorizing the "conceptual unit" alone would seem equivalent to Bhartṛhari's *artha,* the "sound unit" to *dhvani,* and the "mental storehouse of automatically integrated conceptual units" to the *sphoṭas.* But Penfield, along with most other Western thinkers, does not seem to have any notion that such an integrated conceptual unit, or *sphoṭa,* could be an object capable of inner perception, or *pratibhā.* Here is another point on which Bhartṛhari and the whole of Yoga psychology challenges modern thought and research.

The psychological possibility of direct supersensuous intuition of the Divine is one of the major points of divergence between Eastern and Western thought. Bhartṛhari is typically Eastern in maintaining that direct intuition of *Śabdabrahman* is not only possible, but is the necessary means by which the Divine may be known and *mokṣa* realized. In Western thought, the conceiving of intuition on such a high epistemological level has seldom been even suggested, let alone practiced. Perhaps Plato came closest to it in his discussion of the illumination of truth in Book VI of *The Republic.*[32] In more recent times, both Bergson and Spinoza offered intuition as a method of knowing ultimate truth or beauty, which is immediate, certain, and convincing; and can never be refuted or proved by intellect or reason.[33] Contemporary thinkers, such as Bunge, reduce intuition to nothing more than subconscious cases of rapid inference — a view that seems generally accepted by many Western scientists and most psychologists.

Among Western psychologists, Jung's concept of intuition seems to have something in common with Yogic intuition, but he does not accept it as a pure and absolute perception. As a psychological process, Jung finds intuiting to be necessarily subject to modification by thinking, feeling, and sensation, and therefore to be subject to false distortion in its cognitive presentation.[34] For Jung intuition, at the deepest level of the unconscious, is in direct touch with the universal truths of mankind *(archetypes);* but, in its expression in symbolic form at the conscious level, this primitive purity of the intuition is lost. As a means of knowledge, intuition is characterized by Jung as being immediate but uncritical, and this is in complete contrast with the *sphoṭa*/Yoga theorizing where intuition is true and results in right behavior.

It is of interest to note that there is one contemporary psychologist, A. H. Maslow, who has theoretically and experimentally examined a state of consciousness that is in some ways similar to the *pratibhā* of Bhartṛhari. Maslow calls his concept "the cognition of Being in peak-experiences."[35] In such "Being-cognition," says Maslow, the experience or the object tends to be seen as a whole, as a complete unit, detached from relations, from possible usefulness, from expediency, and from purpose. It is seen as if it were all there was in the universe, as if it were all of Being, synonymous with the universe. Maslow finds that for people to have such an experience they must achieve a high level of maturation, health, and self-actualization. They must be able to become egoless to the extent that they can become so absorbed or "poured into" the object that the ego-self in a very real sense disappears. As examples, Maslow examines aesthetic, scientific discovery, and mystical experiences. Maslow also notes that the peak-experience, as he calls it, is self-validating, self-justifying, and carries its own intrinsic value with it. In all of this, Maslow's thinking seems to parallel much of Bhartṛhari's *śabdapūrvayoga*, and perhaps he comes closer than any other Western psychologist to appreciating the transcending of ego required for such intuitive experience. The contribution of Bhartṛhari to Maslow, if a dialogue between the two were rigorously pursued, would be to force Maslow to be more specific as to the function of language and religion in such peak-experiences.

Perhaps Carl Jung is the only modern Western psychologist to agree with Bhartṛhari's contention that consciousness is collective and contains within itself the knowledge of reality. The psyche is defined by Jung as the totality of all conscious as well as unconscious mental processes. For Jung, as for Bhartṛhari, the stuff of consciousness is no less real than the physical matter of the external world. It has an essential dynamism and an ongoing indestructibility.[36] However, Jung's theory of consciousness differs significantly from Bhartṛhari's Yoga in the hierarchical order in which it is conceived. Rather than beginning with consciousness in its most general and most omniscient form (i.e., *Śabdabrahman*), Jung begins with the ego as the dimension of consciousness that in turn is surrounded — in ever expanding concentric circles — by the personal unconscious (containing specific personal acquisitions and forgotten, repressed, or subliminally perceived contents), and by the collective unconscious (which encloses within itself all of the previous dimensions and expands outward in every direction toward infinity). The collective unconscious is based upon the inherited potential for psychic functioning (i.e., neurophysiological structure), out of which contents arise that are common to all humans. It is the foundation for the "primal datum" out of which consciousness ever arises afresh. Consequently, the fundamental human psychic activity is activity of the unconscious. Within it, as within the pervasive Yoga *guṇas* of consciousness, resides the potential dynamics that, when structured by individual growth, represents mankind's universal reactions to typical human situations (fear, hate, sex, love, birth, death, etc.). These are the archetypes.[37]

The Jungian archetypes bear some formal resemblance to the *sphoṭa* (when conceived as an *akliṣṭa saṁskāra* series), in that it is described as a universal and eternal presence that represents the sum of the latent potentialities of the individual psyche. But an idea entirely contrary to the *sphoṭa* conception of its knowledge as pure divine truth occurs when Jung describes the archetypal knowledge as the latent ancestral knowledge of the human race. Thus, for Jung, the knowledge content of consciousness is, at its core (or archetypal level), colored by the darker hues of human passion and cultural history. As Jacobi puts it, "every collective, representing at the same time the sum of its single members, is stamped by the psychic constitution of those members."[38] In the Yoga view of *sphoṭa* within consciousness, however, the knowledge content remains the pure *Śabdabrahman* upon which all lesser levels of human knowledge and language depend. This difference would seem to be a direct outcome of Jung's typically Western, egocentric view of consciousness. For Bhartṛhari, and virtually all other Eastern approaches, the nature of consciousness is primarily identified with God or divine truth — the personal ego being consigned to a relatively low location in the hierarchy of the evolution of consciousness.

Having noted that the archetype in Jung's theory seems to bear some formal resemblance to the *sphoṭa*, it is of interest to see how Jung's conception of the expression of the archetype relates to Bhartṛhari's interpretation of the expression of *sphoṭa*. In agreement with *sphoṭa* theory, Jung conceives of the archetype's external expression as occurring by a process of individuation. Jung calls the external expression a symbol, which may take the form of a word, or more often, a pictorial image. Symbols are never devised consciously but are gradually clarified as the pictorial or word motif moves from the level of the personal consciousness to the deeper level of the collective unconscious. There, says Jung, "the symbol becomes increasingly dominant, for it encloses an archetype, a nucleus of meaning."[39] The archetype would seem to correspond with the *artha* of *sphoṭa* theory, and the pictorial or word form with the *dhvani*.

In Jung's thinking these two aspects, far distant from one another in our psychic functioning, are brought together in the constructive activity of the symbol. The external word form or image is taken deep within consciousness, and unified with a universally valid meaning and power, resulting in a newly created living whole that rises to manifest itself in expression at the level of personal consciousness. This is a process of individuation in that through it the universally shared archetype or meaning nucleus of the collective unconscious becomes limited and expressed within the structures and forms of the individual psyche. But, as was the case in the Yoga interpretation of the *sphoṭa*, this process results in a two-sided psychological dynamic — side by side with the increasing individuation of the collective unconscious into external expression, there is in the reverse direction an increasing integration of the external particulars with the internal universal archetypes. This process is illustrated by Jacobi as follows:

> The first dream of a series, for example, gives a detailed image of the real mother in her limited diurnal role; but gradually the meaning becomes wider and deeper, until the image is transformed into a symbol of Woman in all her variations as the contrasexual partner; then, rising up from a still deeper stratum, the image discloses mythological features, becomes a fairy or a dragon; in the deepest stratum, the storehouse of collective, universally human experience, it takes the form of a dark cave, the underworld, the ocean, and finally it swells into the one half of creation, chaos, the darkness that receives and conceives.[40]

The manifestation of an integrated symbol occurs, says Jung, as an intuition or revelation, and thus seems very near to the *sphoṭa pratibhā*. Such symbols are described by Jung as growing up from the dark depths of the mind, and forming a most important part of the subliminal psyche. For evidence of this, Jung observes how, in everyday life, dilemmas are solved by surprising new propositions that appear suddenly from the unconscious. Artists, philosophers, and even scientists owe some of their best ideas to inspirations that appear suddenly from the unconscious. Jung cites the examples of Poincare, the mathematician, and Kekule, the chemist (structure of benzene molecule), who themselves describe their scientific discoveries in terms of sudden "revelations" from the unconscious. In the field of literature the experience of Robert Louis Stevenson is recounted. After spending several years looking for a story to fit his "strong sense of man's double being," the plot of *Dr. Jekyll and Mr. Hyde* was suddenly revealed to him in a dream. Such dream symbolism, notes Jung, is especially potent because new images are expressed that have not yet reached the level of consciousness.[41]

Although Jung is helpful in his analysis of the relevance of Eastern concepts of intuition for modernity, his psychology remains rather vague in the precise details as to exactly how the archetype becomes individuated through the various levels of consciousness to its integrated expression in thought and speech. The Yoga analysis seems in many ways to be more detailed and thoroughgoing. Aside from this, there appears to be a definite difference of emphasis in Jung's approach when compared with the individuation of Yoga. For Jung the end goal seems to be conceived as the individually created integration of the universalized archetypal meaning at the ego-conscious level of thought and speech *(madhyamā* and *vaikharī vāk).* For Bhartṛhari, however, the dualistic expression of *vāk* is useful only as the means for achieving that *paśyantī* state in which there is no subject-object separation but only the direct experience of the *sphoṭa* as the uncreated and divinely given meaning-whole within consciousness. Whereas Jung's emphasis is on the humanly created individuation, Bhartṛhari's focus is on the reintegration of individuated expressions *(citta vṛttis)* until egoity vanishes and all that remains is the unitary universal unconsciousness that is *Śabdabrahman.* Bhartṛhari's challenge to Jung and to other Western psychologists is that unless the "ego-knot" is untied, the light of metaphysical knowledge, aesthetic experience, and religious realization will not be experienced.[42]

The relating of Bhartṛhari to recent Western aesthetics has not yet been thoroughly attempted, although V. K. Chari is making helpful contributions in this regard. Chari sees the Western reaction as a tendency to dismiss the notion of an inner *sphoṭa* or *rasadhvani* as mere subjectivism or mysticism. Indian aesthetics, following Bhartṛhari, can respond by pointing out that although the inner aesthetic may be individual in experience, it has its foundation in universal human consciousness. In this sense the aesthetic experience is not so much subjective as intersubjective. Chari concludes, "Without assuming such an affinity of nature between the poet and reader on the one hand, and between a community of readers on the other, no aesthetic communication would be conceivable."[43] This seems similar to Immanuel Kant's understanding of the universal but subjective nature of aesthetic judgment as outlined in his *Critique of Judgement*. The contribution of Bhartṛhari to the modern literary critics may well be his forceful demonstration of the need for all aesthetic experience to be grounded in a common universal consciousness such as *Śabdabrahman*.

In the final analysis, however, Bhartṛhari's most important contribution to modern life may well be in the field of religious experience. It is Bhartṛhari's understanding of language as revelation of the Divine that continues to fascinate this author. At a time when the sacred scriptures of all traditions are losing their depth and power as a result of being interpreted as strictly the product of human imagination, Bhartṛhari comes as a fresh breath of the Divine Spirit. Rather than trusting in the methods of science, reason, and historical analysis to take one to the essence of the Divine, Bhartṛhari counsels trust in and deep meditation upon the revealed word itself. Many today who are attempting to be sincerely spiritual find that their scriptures no longer speak powerfully to them of God. Instead, under the conditioning of scientific literary criticism, the scripture often reveals only human things: by whom was it written, at what date, in what social and political circumstance, and so on. Bhartṛhari's teaching for the modern spiritual seeker is that the revealed words are to be meditated upon, not only with reference to surrounding historical circumstances *(vaikharī vāk)* and logical rationality *(madhyamā vāk)*, but with openness to the divine vision within *(paśyantī vāk)*. When such an approach to the study of scripture is taken, and the divine spirit embodied within the words is allowed to work in one's consciousness, the result is spiritual sanctification of the highest order *(śabdapūrvayoga)*.

The need for this is clearly evidenced in the modern fascination for any meditational technique that will raise one beyond the levels of empirical or rational consciousness. The message of Bhartṛhari for the modern age is a religious message. That altered (higher) state of consciousness you are seeking is already present within language itself. But its higher levels are known only through the special language of scriptural revelation. Meditate on these Divine Words, with no thought for yourself or your own knowledge of them. Let your consciousness be filled with their truth and power, and the ultimate religious experience of knowing God will be yours.

Notes and References

Chronology

1. This play is mentioned by K. A. Subramania Iyer in his excellent study of the *Vākyapadīya* entitled *Bhartṛhari*, p. 1.

2. The writings of the Buddhist scholars I-tsing, Diṅnāga, and Vasubandhu have been carefully analyzed in terms of their relationship to Bhartṛhari by the following: J. Takakusu, H. R. Rangaswamy Iyengar, M. Winternitz, H. Ui, E. Frauwallner, S. Yamaguchi, and H. Nakamura. This long-standing technical scholarly debate is nicely summarized by Hajime Nakamura in his "Tibetan Citations of Bhartṛhari's Verses and the Problem of His Date" in *Studies in Indology and Buddhology* (Kyoto: Hozokan, 1955).

3. *Ibid.*, p. 132.

4. *Ibid.*, p. 133.

5. See conclusion of H. Nakamura, *ibid.*, p. 135, and that of K. A. Subramania Iyer in his *Bhartṛhari*, p. 2.

6. This list is based upon the scholarly research of K. A. Subramania Iyer, who carefully examines the evidence and argues for Bhartṛhari's authorship of these works in *Bhartṛhari*, pp. 4–15.

Chapter One

1. For a helpful map of the Gupta Empire at the close of the fourth century A.D. see *The Oxford Pictorial Atlas of Indian History*, edited by K. Srinivas Kini and U. Bhavani Shanker Rao (Oxford: Oxford University Press, 1967), pp. 12–14.

2. For example, Fa Hian reached India ca. A.D. 401, and from that time onward a steady stream of scholars and pilgrims crossed the desert in search of knowledge, and brought back to China manuscripts, relics, and statues that had a lasting effect on Chinese culture. H. G. Rawlinson, *India: A Short Cultural History*, (London: Cresset Press, 1965), p. 144.

3. These and the above-made statements regarding the social, economic, and educational state of the people are based upon *An Advanced History of India* by R. C. Majumdar, H. G. Raychauduri, and Kalikinkar Datta, 3rd ed. (London: Macmillan, 1967), pp. 188–92.

4. Daniel H. Ingalls, "Sanskrit Poetry and Sanskrit Poetics," a paper read at the Indiana University Conference on Oriental-Western Literary Relations, n.d., pp. 1–2.

5. *Ibid.*, pp. 7–8, 10.

6. For a detailed description of the golden age of Sanskrit under the Guptas as evidenced in Kālidāsa, see B. S. Upadhyaya, *India in Kālidāsa* (Delhi: S. Chand and Co., 1968); reference to Samudra Gupta and Skanda Gupta on pp. 88–89.

7. See the preface to the *Vaīragya-Śatakam of Bhartṛhari*, edited by Swami Gambhirananda, p. i.

8. K. Krishnamoorthy, "Traditional Indian Aesthetics in Theory and Practice," in *Indian Aesthetics and Art Activity* (Simla: Indian Institute of Advanced Study, 1968), p. 43.

9. *Ibid.*

10. See N. K. Brahma, *The Philosophy of Hindu Sādhanā* (London: Kegan Paul, Trench, Truber, 1932).

11. See R. C. Dutt, *Later Hindu Civilization* (Calcutta: Punthi Pustak, 1965), pp. 58–64.

12. See, for example, *Ṛg Veda* 10.10.114.8 (*yāvad brahma viṣṭhītam tavatī vāk,* the loom of speech is writ large over the whole creation).

13. *Ṛg Veda* 10.10.125.3.

14. *Ibid.*, 10.10.114.8.

15. *Ibid.*, 5.10.2 and 10.114.8.

16. *Bṛihadāraṇyaka Upaniṣad* 4.1.2.

17. *John* 1:1 and *Genesis* 1.

18. T. R. V. Murti, "Some Thoughts on the Indian Philosophy of Language." Presidential Address to the 37th Indian Philosophical Congress, 1963, p. viii.

19. Aurobindo Ghose, *On the Veda* (Pondicherry: Sri Aurobindo Ashram Press, 1956), p. 6.

20. J. G. Arapura, "Language and Phenomena," *Canadian Journal of Theology*, XVI, 1 and 2 (1970), p. 44.

21. *Taittiriya Upaniṣad* 1.8.1.

22. From the viewpoint of Brāhmanical teaching, the psychological functioning of an individual includes a sixth sense in addition to the five accepted in modern thinking (i.e., sight, sound, smell, touch, and taste) — the sixth sense organ being the mind, which perceives ideas or knowledge directly, intuitively. This view of the mind was also shared by Jainism and Buddhism, and is still taught in Eastern psychology (Yoga) to the present day. In popular or commonsense contemporary thought it is present as for example in the cartoon representation of a character "seeing" a light bulb flash in his mind, revealing an insight or idea.

23. D. M. Datta, *The Six Ways of Knowing*, pp. 20–27.

24. *Sāṅkhya Kārikā of Īśvara Krishna*, translated by J. Davies (Calcutta: Susil Gupta, 1947), *kārikā* 4.

25. Ganganatha Jha, *Pūrva-Mīmāṁsā* in Its Sources, p. 80. Prabhākara accepts only five *pramāṇas*.

26. Dharmarāja Adhvarin, *Vedānta Paribhāṣā*, translated by S. S. Sastri (Adhyar: Adyar Library and Research Center, 1942), chs. 1–6.

27. *Sāṅkhya Aphorisms of Kapila,* translated by J. R. Ballantyne, 4th ed. (Varanasi: Chowkhamba Sanskrit Series, 1963), bk. I, aph. 101.

28. See, for example, the distinction made between general and special revelation in *A Handbook of Christian Theology*, edited by M. Halverson and A. Cohen (New York: World, 1958), pp. 327–28.

29. *Patañjali's Yoga Sūtras* with the commentary of Vyāsa and the gloss of Vācaspati Miśra, translated by Rāma Prasāda, 3rd ed. (Allahabad: Bhuvaneswari Asrama, 1924), I:25–27.

30. These statements are based on the *Shabara Bhāṣya* as translated by Ganganatha Jha in *Pūrva-Mīmāṁsā in Its Sources*, pp. 97–98.

31. *Mīmāṁsā Sūtras of Jaimini* and the *Bhāṣya* of Śabara, as translated by Ganganatha Jha in *Pūrva-Mīmāṁsā in Its Sources, sūtra* 12.

32. *Ibid., sūtra* 23.

33. *Śabara Bhāṣya,* in Jha, *Pūrva-Mīmāṁsā in Its Sources,* p. 99.

34. Śaṅkara, *The Vedānta Sūtras*, translated by G. Thibaut (Delhi: Motilal Banarsidass, 1962), I.3.30, pp. 211–16.

35. *Ibid.*, I.3.28, p. 204.

36. *Ibid.*, 4.1.3.

37. The Advaita Vedānta central tenet of the nonduality of Brahman raises many thorny issues when considered in relation to *śabda*. For example, *śabda* is held by Śaṅkara to be eternal. Thus it would seem that there are two eternal entities coexisting, Brahman and *śabda*, but this is unacceptable when Brahman is defined as "absolute nonduality." Then again it is held that Brahman alone is real and that truth is made known by *śabda*. Now, is *śabda*, which is evidence for Brahman, real or unreal? If it is real, then there is a reality other than Brahman. If it is unreal, then Brahman, which is its content, cannot be real. For the Advaitin such dilemmas are resolved by holding that, on the phenomenal side, there are various levels in our perception of truth. Ultimately, however, nondual Brahman is the only absolute, and the unreality of *śabda* is accepted.

38. It should be noted here that although the Nyāya and Vaiśeṣikas are traditionally classed as orthodox Brāhmanical schools, on the question of *śabda pramāṇa* they stand somewhere in between the divine and the conventional viewpoints. The Nyāya, for example, takes *śabda* to be neither impersonal nor self-evidently valid. It maintains that the Vedas are created by God, but that notwithstanding such divine authorship, their validity ultimately must be proved by perception or inference. For a concise presentation of this position along with a discussion of the Jaina and Vaiśeṣika viewpoints, see S. Chatterjee, *The Nyāya Theory of Knowledge*, pp. 319–21.

39. Mādhava Āchārya, *Sarva-Darśana-Saṃgraha,* translated by E. B. Cowell and A. E. Gough, 6th ed. (Varanasi: Chowkamba Sanskrit Series, 1961) pp. 2–11.

40. Dale Riepe, *The Naturalistic Tradition in Indian Thought* (Seattle: University of Washington Press, 1961), p. 66.

41. *Ibid.*, p. 127.

42. Gopinath Kaviraj, "The Doctrine of Pratibhā in Indian Philosophy," *Annals of the Bhandarkar Oriental Research Institute* (1924), p. 122.

43. K. N. Jayatilleke, *Early Buddhist Theory of Knowledge* (London: Allen and Unwin, 1963), p. 183.

44. *Ibid.*, p. 185.

45. *Vākyapadīya of Bhartṛhari*, translated by K. A. Subramania Iyer, I:123. Related to this point is the Grammar school's rejection of gestures as independent vehicles for communicating meaning. As Punyarāja puts it, the shaking of the head indicating negation does not communicate independent of words. The gesture serves to make one think of the word "no" before it can communicate the meaning of negation or refusal. P. K. Chakravarti, *The Linguistic Speculations of the Hindus*, p. 72.

46. Edward Sapir, *Language* (New York: Harcourt, Brace and World, 1949), p. 15.

47. T. R. V. Murti, "Some Thoughts on the Indian Philosophy of Language," p. iii.

Chapter Two

1. As reported in *The History and Culture of the Indian People: The Classical Age*, edited by R. C. Majumdar (Bombay: Bharatiya Vidya Bhavan, 1962) pp. 586–89.

2. Tradition has consistently maintained Bhartṛhari's authorship; however, some contemporary scholars, notably M. Biardeau, argue against this tradition and attempt to ascribe the *vṛtti* to Harivṛṣabha. K. A. Subramania Iyer has carefully reviewed both sides of this argument and concludes that with the evidence now available, Bhartṛhari should still be taken as the author of both the *kārikās* and the *vṛtti*. See *Bhartṛhari*, pp. 16–36.

3. These problems are given full discussion by K. A. S. Iyer in *Bhartṛhari*, pp. 6–9. He has also translated ch. III, pt. i into English. The *kārikās* only of ch. II have been put into English by K. Raghavan Pillai, *The Vākyapadīya* (Delhi: Motilal Banarsidass, 1971).

4. Translation by T. R. V. Murti, *Some Thoughts on the Indian Philosophy of Language*, p. 10.

5. *Ibid.*, p. 11.

6. *Ibid.*, p. 12.

7. *Sarva-Darśana-Saṃgraha*, translated by E. B. Cowell and A. E. Gough, p. 219.

8. T. R. V. Murti, *Some Thoughts on the Indian Philosophy of Language*, pp. 14–15.

9. *Sarva-Darśana-Saṃgraha*, p. 211.

10. Gaurinath Sastri, *The Philosophy of Word and Meaning*, pp. 102–03.

11. V. S. Apte, *The Practical Sanskrit-English Dictionary*, 3rd ed. (Delhi: Motilal Banarsidass, 1965), p. 1013.
12. *Vākyapadīya of Bhartṛhari*, translated by K. A. Subramania Iyer, I:5–10.
13. *Ibid.*, I:44.
14. *Ibid.*, I:45–46.
15. This and the following statements are based upon K. A. S. Iyer's excellent summary of Bhartṛhari's theory in *Bhartṛhari*, pp. 90–91 and 177–80.
16. *Vākyapadīya*, I:47–49.
17. T. S. Eliot, "Burnt Norton," in *A Little Treasury of Modern Poetry*, edited by Oscar Williams (New York: Scribner's, 1952), p. 294.
18. *Vākyapadīya*, *vṛtti* on I:51.
19. *Ibid.*, *vṛtti* on I:1.
20. *Ibid.*, *vṛtti* on I:24–26.
21. *Ibid.*, especially the second chapter in which he establishes the *vākya* or sentence *sphoṭa* over against the view of the Mīmāṁsakas.
22. *Ibid.*, II:153 ff.
23. *Sphoṭasiddhi of Maṇḍana Miśra*, translated by K. A. Subramania Iyer.
24. *Ślokāvartika by Kumārilabhāṭṭa*, translated by Ganganatha Jha, *sūtra* V, section 12, pp. 261–68.
25. *Sphoṭasiddhi*, p. 3.
26. *Ibid.*, *sūtra* 19. Similar arguments are offered to show how the progressively clearer perception cannot be attributed to defects of the senses or memory through resemblance.
27. *Vākyapadīya*, *vṛtti* on I:88.
28. *Ibid.*, I:142.
29. *Ibid.*, I:123.
30. A thoughtful criticism of this position has been offered by Jayantabhaṭṭa in his *Nyāyamañjari*. The main point of his criticism seems to be that Bhartṛhari is misled when he identifies word and consciousness and takes this so-called *Śabdabrahman* as both the efficient and the material cause of knowledge. Jayanta's argument is that words simply illuminate objects that already exist — the word is not at once the illuminator and the object, otherwise what is it that the word denotes? Then again, says Jayanta, all cognition is not necessarily determinative or verbal in nature. In fact, in experience we first cognize the object and only then is a word roused up and used to signify it. See G. N. Shastri, "The Doctrine of Śabdabrahman — A Criticism by Jayantabhaṭṭa," *Indian Historical Quarterly*, XV, 441–53. Jayanta's position would seem to lead into an infinite regress, however, in attempting to explain why a particular word should be roused up in response to a particular object. To invoke memory only lands one in the same dilemma one step farther back. At some point, it would seem some natural fitness or self-revelation on the part of *śabda* is inevitable, if communication is to be logically explained.

31. *Vākyapadīya,* I:3.
32. Iyer, *Bhartṛhari,* p. 118.
33. Eliot, "Burnt Norton," in *A Little Treasury of Modern Poetry,* p. 289.
34. *Vākyapadīya,* I:11–12.
35. Iyer, *Bhartṛhari,* p. 68.
36. *Ibid.,* p. 108.
37. *Vākyapadīya,* II:146–50.
38. Sastri, *Philosophy of Word and Meaning,* pp. 66–82.
39. For a discussion of this point from the Kashmir Śaivism perspective, see K. C. Pandey, *Abhinavagupta,* p. 260 ff.
40. K. Sivaraman, *Śaivism in Philosophical Perspective* (Varanasi: Motilal Banarsidass, 1972), pp. 223–29.
41. *Vākyapadīya,* I:16.
42. *Ibid., vṛtti* on I:5. K. A. S. Iyer finds that although *granthi* usually has the meaning of transformation *(vikāra),* Bhartṛhari consistently uses it as the *karmic* habit patterns *(vāsanā)* that cause phenomenalization.
43. *Vākyapadīya, vṛtti* on I:130 (Iyer's numbering, I:122 in other manuscripts).
44. Iyer, *Bhartṛhari,* p. 141.
45. *Ibid.,* p. 145.
46. *Ibid.,* p. 404.

Chapter Three

1. *The Yoga System of Patañjali,* translated by J. H. Woods (Delhi: Motilal Banarsidass, 1966; also vol. 17 of Harvard Oriental Series). *Patañjali's Yoga Sūtras,* translated by Rāma Prasāda; vol. 4, *The Sacred Books of the Hindus.* The English of James H. Woods, although very literal, does not always convey an understanding of the Sanskrit. Rāma Prasāda's translation gives one a much better sense of what the Sanskrit intends. In his preface James Woods includes a discussion of the dating of the work; however, since his time scholarship has generally pushed all the dates back to a century or so earlier than Woods indicates.
2. Jadunath Sinha, *Indian Psychology: Cognition* (Calcutta: Sinha Publishing House, 1958), ch. 17.
3. T. H. Stcherbatsky, *The Conception of Buddhist Nirvāṇa* (London: Mouton, 1965), pp. 16–19.
4. Mircea Eliade, *Yoga: Immortality and Freedom* (Princeton: Princeton University Press, 1958), p. 3. The other three motifs named by Eliade are *karma, māyā,* and *nirvāṇa.*
5. K. A. S. Iyer, *Bhartṛhari,* and Gaurinath Sastri, *The Philosophy of Word and Meaning.* Another contemporary scholar, K. Kunjunni Raja, recognizes the importance of the psychological side of Bhartṛhari's thought, but analyzes it in terms of modern European associationalist psychology — a theory completely foreign to Bhartṛhari's thought and the thought forms of his day. See his *Indian Theories of Meaning.*

6. *Patañjali's Yoga Sūtras,* I:24–29.
7. *Ibid.,* I:24–25.
8. *Ibid.,* II:18, *bhāṣya.*
9. *Ibid.,* I:26.
10. *Ibid.,* I:25.
11. *Ibid.,* I:24.
12. Iyer, *Bhartṛhari,* pp. 90–93. As Iyer has observed, this parallel was noticed by Helārāja, who quotes from Vyāsa's commentary on *Yoga Sūtra* 1:25 in this context.
13. *Yoga Sūtras,* I:24, *ṭīkā.*
14. In all experience of self-consciousness or thinking, this metaphysical assumption of wrong identification between *puruṣa* and *prakṛti* is held to obtain. Since the present concern is with the psychology of thinking, and not the ultimate nature of the metaphysics involved, the discussion proceeds as if the *sattva* aspect of *prakṛti* were indeed real consciousness or illumination. This is in accord with the Yoga view of the nature of psychological processes at the thinking level. The *sattva* aspect of the thinking substance *(citta),* insofar as it is absolutely clear, takes on or reflects the intelligence *(cāitanya)* of *puruṣa.* For practical purposes, therefore, no duality appears, and *prakṛti* may be treated as self-illuminating (see *ṭīkā* [explanation] on *Yoga Sūtra* I:17).
15. S. N. Dasgupta finds that both the *Yoga Sūtras* and the *Vākyapadīya* adopt a kind of commonsense identification or ontological unity between the whole (the universal) and the parts (the particular manifestations). The three *guṇas* are the one universal genus, and it is the *guṇas* in various collocations that show themselves as the particular manifestations. *Yoga Philosophy* (Calcutta: University of Calcutta, 1930) pp. 120–26.
16. *Yoga Sūtras,* III:9.
17. *Ibid.,* I:5.
18. *Ibid.,* I:12.
19. *Ibid.,* II:4–6.
20. *Ibid.,* I:18, *ṭīkā.*
21. *Vākyapadīya, vṛtti* on I:51.
22. *Ibid., vṛtti* on I:1.
23. *Yoga Sūtras,* II:19, *bhāṣya.* Although for our present purpose the inherent knowledge aspect of the *buddhitattva* is the point of focus, it should be realized that the *buddhitattva,* as the collective of all the individual minds *(buddhi)* with their beginningless *saṁskāras* of ignorance *(avidyā)* from previous births, also contains within it the inherent *avidyā* of the individual souls. And from the viewpoint of language, this *avidyā* would be composed of all the residual traces of the use of words in previous lives *(śabdabhāvanā).* See also Iyer, *Bhartṛhari,* p. 91.
24. S. N. Dasgupta, *The Study of Patañjali* (Calcutta: University of Calcutta, 1920), p. 53.
25. Iyer, *Bhartṛhari,* p. 149.

26. S. N. Dasgupta, *A History of Indian Philosophy* (Cambridge: The University Press, 1932), I, 250.
27. Dasgupta, *Yoga Philosophy*, p. 209.
28. *Yoga Sūtras*, III:41.
29. *Vākyapadīya*, II:117–18 and I:122.
30. *Ibid.*, I:46–47 and I:142.
31. *Ibid.*, I:84, *vṛtti*.
32. *Yoga Sūtras*, *bhāṣya* on III:17.
33. *Ibid.*, III:41, *ṭīkā*.
34. *Ibid.*, III:17, *ṭīkā*. See also *Vākyapadīya* I:84.
35. *Ibid.*, III:17, *bhāṣya*.
36. Iyer, *Bhartṛhari*, pp. 205–07 and 372. Bhartṛhari shows this superimposition to hold at all levels of linguistic complexity and offers the example of the appearance of the whole meaning in each part of the *dvandva* compound.
37. *Yoga Sūtras*, III:17, *bhāṣya*.
38. *Ibid.*, *ṭīkā*.
39. *Ibid.*, *bhāṣya*.
40. *Vākyapadīya*, II:73.
41. *Ibid.*, I:142, *vṛtti*.
42. *Yoga Sūtras* I:44.
43. *Vākyapadīya*, I:153–55.
44. *Ibid.*, I:131, *vṛtti*. It should be noted that while this interpretation is based on *Yoga Sūtras* I:12–16, only one aspect of Yoga *vairāgya* is represented — the turning away of the mind from all forms of worldly attachment. For Pantañjali's Yoga at its ultimate level, *vairāgya* also involves the turning away of the mind from all forms of *vāk* so that the "seeded" or *samprajñāta samādhi* gives way to a "nonseeded" or "nonword" *asamprajñāta* state. (See *Yoga Sūtras* I:50–51 and II:15 ff.). For Bhartṛhari, since consciousness is shot through with *vāk*, *samādhi* in its highest elevations will always be "seeded" with Vedic word (see *Vākyapadīya* I:123).
45. *Vākyapadīya* II:28, *bhāṣya*.
46. *Ibid.*, II:30, *bhāṣya*.
47. See Jacob Needleman, *The New Religions* (Richmond Hill: Simon and Schuster, 1972), and William McNamara, *The Human Adventure: Contemplation for Everyman* (New York: Doubleday, 1974).
48. *Vākyapadīya*, I:14.
49. *Yoga Sūtras*, II:49–52.
50. *Ibid.*, II:47, *bhāṣya* and *ṭīkā*, and II:48.
51. *Ibid.*, II:50–53.
52. As quoted in Eliade, *Yoga: Immortality and Freedom*, pp. 55–56.
53. *Vākyapadīya*, I:131, *vṛtti*.
54. *Yoga Sūtras*, III:4.
55. Dasgupta, *Yoga Philosophy*, p. 335.
56. *Yoga-Sāra-Saṅgraha of Vijñana Bhikṣu*, translated by Ganganatha Jha (Madras: Theosophical Publishing House, 1932), p. 88.

57. *Yoga Sūtras,* III:2.
58. *Ibid.,* III:3, *bhāṣya.*
59. *Ibid.,* III:5.
60. *Ibid.,* I:42–44.
61. *Ibid.,* I:43, *ṭīkā.*
62. *Ibid.,* I:44, *bhāṣya.*
63. *Vākyapadīya,* II:152.
64. Iyer, *Bhartṛhari,* p. 90.

Chapter Four

1. See for example, K. C. Pandey, *Comparative Aesthetics,* vols. I and II; S. K. De, *History of Sanskrit Poetics,* vols. I and II, 2nd ed. (Calcutta: K. L. Mukhopadhyay, 1960); and P. V. Kane, *History of Sanskrit Poetics,* 4th ed. (Delhi: Motilal Banarsidass, 1971). *Rasa* (the dominant emotional mood) is another central notion that appears to be intimately related to *dhvani.* Other common notions include: *doṣas* (flaws), *alamkāras* (figures of speech), *rīti* (style), *guṇas* (special qualities).
2. *Dhvanyāloka of Anandavardhana,* translated by K. Krishnamoorthy, I:13, p. 9. This important work on Indian aesthetics is dated ca. A.D. 850 in Kashmir.
3. *Vālmīki Rāmāyaṇa* as quoted in translation by K. C. Pandey, 260–61.
4. *Ibid.,* p. 263.
5. *Vākyapadīya,* I:5.
6. *Ibid.,* I:44–48.
7. Nāgeśa Bhaṭṭa, *Sphoṭavada* (Madras: Adyar Library, 1946), p. 5.
8. William Shakespeare, *The Works of William Shakespeare* (London: Frederick Warne and Co., 1893), sonnet 116, p. 1110.
9. Tarapada Chakrabarti, *Indian Aesthetics and Science of Language* (Calcutta: Sanskrit Pustak Bhandar, 1971), p. 146.
10. *Vakyapadīya,* I:47.
11. *Dhvanyāloka,* I:13, *vṛtti,* p. 14.
12. A. Sankaran, *Some Aspects of Literary Criticism in Sanskrit,* p. 66.
13. *Ibid.*
14. *Dhvanyāloka,* I:13, p. 9.
15. De, *History of Sanskrit Poetics,* I, 16.
16. Kane, *History of Sanskrit Poetics,* p. 356.
17. S. D. De, "The Theory of Rasa in Sanskrit Poetics," *Sir Asutosh Mookerjee Silver Jubilee Volumes,* (Calcutta: Calcutta University, 1921), vol. 3, pt. 2, p. 218.
18. *Ibid.,* p. 219.
19. P. C. Lahiri, *Concepts of Rīti and Guṇa in Sanskrit Poetics,* pp. 85–90.
20. Sankaran, *Some Aspects of Literary Criticism,* p. 79. For a detailed analysis of how Ananda's *dhvani* encompasses and supersedes all previous aesthetic theories, see pp. 79–84.
21. For a detailed presentation of Abhinavagupta's aesthetic theory see K. C. Pandey, *Comparative Aesthetics,* vol. I.

22. Although a Western reader can follow this move in terms of its logic — i.e., from the level of the phenomenal or conditioned to the universal or unconditioned — he will not perceive the total implication for the Eastern mind until some grasp of the underlying psychology is also attained. See Chapter 3 and the following sections of this chapter.

23. Pandey, *Comparative Aesthetics,* p. 140.

24. Sankaran, *Some Aspects of Literary Criticism,* p. 116.

25. De, "The Theory of Rasa in Sanskrit Poetics," p. 222.

26. Sankaran, *Some Aspects of Literary Criticism,* pp. 132–36.

27. *Vākyapadīya,* II:143–45.

28. A. E. Houseman, in *A Little Treasury of Modern Poetry* (New York: Scribner's, 1952), p. xxxvi.

29. Sankaran, *Some Aspects of Literary Criticism,* p. 104.

30. *Patañjali's Yoga Sūtras,* II:19, *bhāṣya.*

31. See K. H. Pribram, "The Neurophysiology of Remembering," *Scientific American,* January 1969, pp. 73–86, and K. H. Pribram, "Neurological Notes on Knowing," Proceedings of Second Banff Conference on Theoretical Psychology, Banff, 1969.

32. Pribram, "Neurological Notes on Knowing," p. 16.

33. "The Recording of Consciousness and the Function of the Interpretive Cortex," in *Speech and Brain-Mechanisms,* by W. Penfield and L. Roberts (Princeton: Princeton University Press, 1959) pp. 38–55.

34. Jolande Jacobi, *The Psychology of C. G. Jung* (New Haven: Yale University Press, 1958), p. 5.

35. *Ibid.,* p. 2.

36. Ruth Monroe, *Schools of Psychoanalytic Thought* (New York: Dryden Press, 1955), p. 541.

37. Jacobi, *Psychology of C. G. Jung,* pp. 43–48.

38. *Ibid.,* p. 92.

39. C. R. Peterson and L. R. Beach, "Man as an Intuitive Statistician," *Psychological Bulletin,* 68 (1967), pp. 42–43.

Chapter Five

1. "Nītiśataka," *sloka* 2, translated by B. S. Miller in *Bhartṛhari: Poems* (New York: Columbia University Press, 1967).

2. M. R. Kale, *The Nīti and Vairāgya Śatakas of Bhartṛhari* (Delhi: Motilal Banarsidass, 1902).

3. D. D. Kosambi, "The Epigrams Attributed to Bhartṛhari," *Singhi Jain Series,* 23, (1948), and "On the Authorship of the Satakatrayī," *Journal of Oriental Research,* 15 (Madras, 1946), pp. 64–77.

4. See K. A. S. Iyer's careful discussion of this problem in his *Bhartṛhari,* pp. 10–12. Although Iyer agrees with Kosambi that we cannot definitely know who the author of the *Śatakas* was, Iyer finds no evidence that contradicts the traditional identification of Bhartṛhari the poet with Bhartṛhari the grammarian.

5. Wm. Theodore de Bary, foreword to Miller, *Bhartṛhari: Poems.*
6. Miller, *Bhartṛhari: Poems,* introduction, p. xxvii.
7. *Patañjali's Yoga Sūtras,* II:3–9 with Vyāsa's *bhāṣya* and Vācaspati Miśra's *ṭīkā.*
8. *Ibid.,* II:4.
9. *Ibid.,* II:5.
10. References to the *Vairāgya-Śataka* are to the *sloka* numbering in the Advaita Ashrama edition, Calcutta, 1963. The translations are by B. S. Miller unless otherwise noted.
11. *Yoga Sūtras* II:6.
12. *Ibid.,* II:7.
13. *Vairāgya-Śataka,* Advaita Ashrama commentary on *sloka* 17, p. 11.
14. *Yoga Sūtras* II:8.
15. W. B. Yeats, "Sailing to Byzantium," in *A Little Treasury of Modern Poetry,* edited by Oscar Williams (New York: Scribner's, 1952) p. 69.
16. *Vairāgya-Śataka, sloka* 9, p. 6.
17. *Yoga Sūtras* II:9.
18. *Ibid.,* I:12, *bhāṣya.*
19. *Ibid.,* I:15.
20. *Ibid.,* II:28.
21. *Ibid.,* II:29.
22. *Ibid.,* II:30.
23. *Ibid.,* II:34.
24. *Vairāgya-Śataka, sloka* 14, p. 9.
25. *Yoga Sūtras* II:32.
26. *Ibid.,* II:32.
27. *Vairāgya-Śataka, sloka* 77, p. 44.
28. *Yoga Sūtras* II:32, *bhāṣya.*
29. *Vairāgya-Śataka, slokas* 83 and 84, p. 48.
30. *Yoga Sūtras* II:32.
31. *Vairāgya-Śataka, sloka* 82.
32. *Yoga Sūtras* II:34, *bhāṣya.*
33. *Ibid.,* II:46.
34. *Vairāgya-Śataka, sloka* 85, p. 49.
35. *Ibid.,* see, e.g., *slokas* 89, 95, and 100.
36. *Ibid., sloka* 63, p. 37.
37. *Yoga Sūtras* III:4.
38. *Ibid., bhāṣya* on III:3.
39. *Ibid.,* I:44, *bhāṣya.*

Chapter Six

1. *Ṛg Veda* X:125:3–5, translation by Griffith in *A Sourcebook of Indian Philosophy,* edited by S. Radhakrishnan and C. A. Moore (Princeton: Princeton University Press, 1967), pp. 15–16.

2. William James, *The Varieties of Religious Experience* (New York: Mentor, 1958), pp. 112–206.
3. *Ibid.*, pp. 76–111.
4. *Bṛihadāranyaka Upaniṣad* 2:5:19.
5. *Śvetāśvatara Upaniṣad* 4:8–9.
6. *Bhagavad-Gītā* 7:13–14.
7. *Brahma-Sūtra-Śaṅkara-Bhāṣya*, translated by V. M. Apte, II.1.14, pp. 303–04.
8. *Ibid.*, I.3.28.
9. See K. S. Murty, *Revelation and Reason in Advaita Vedānta*, pp. 40–50, for a helpful and clear summary of the arguments on this point.
10. *Brahma-Sūtra-Śaṅkara-Bhāṣya*, 1.3.28.
11. *Ibid.*, 1.1.5.
12. *The Pancapādikā of Padmapāda*, translated by D. Venkataramiah (Baroda: Oriental Institute, 1948) p. xiii.
13. *Ibid.*, 6.16.
14. *Ibid.*, 15.49.
15. *The Tattvasaṅgraha of Śāntarakṣīta* with the commentary of Kamalaśīla, translated by Ganganatha Jha (Baroda: Oriental Institute, 1937), vol. I, ch. v.
16. For a clear presentation of these Buddhist philosophies in English see T. R. V. Murti, *The Central Philosophy of Buddhism.*
17. That this contention is well founded is evidenced by the fact that both the Hindu scholar K. A. S. Iyer, *Bhartṛhari*, p. 2, and the Buddhist scholar H. Nakamura, "Tibetan Citations of Bhartṛhari's Verses and the Problem of His Date" in *Studies in Indology and Buddhology* (Kyoto: Hozokan, 1955), p. 135, subscribe to it.
18. For more on the Kashmir development of Bhartṛhari see *The Philosophy of Word and Meaning* by Gaurinath Sastri, ch. 4.
19. *The Century of Life of Bhartṛhari*, translated into English verse by Aurobindo Ghose (Pondicherry: Sri Aurobindo Ashram, 1969).
20. Iyer, *Bhartṛhari*, p. 402.
21. W. M. Urban, *Language and Reality* (London: Allen and Unwin, 1939) pp. 21–22.
22. See, for example, ch. 13, "The Word Unit: The Incorporative Capacity of Language," in Wilhelm von Humboldt's *Linguistic Variability and Intellectual Development*, translated by G. C. Buch and F. A. Raven (Florida: University of Miami Press, 1971).
23. K. M. Max Müller, *The Six Systems of Indian Philosophy* (London: Longmans, Green and Co., 1899), and *Lectures on the Science of Language* (Delhi: Munski Ram Manohar Lal, 1861; reprint, 1965).
24. E. Cassirer, *Language and Myth*, translated by S. Langer (New York: Dover, 1946). This work, which evidences considerable influence from the Indian concept of speech *(vāk)*, formed the basis for much of the thinking upon which his *Philosophy of Symbolic Forms* depends (see translator's preface, p. vii ff.)

25. Noam Chomsky, *Language and Mind* (New York: Harcourt, Brace and World, 1968), p. 76.

26. William James, *Psychology* (New York: Holt and Co., 1893), p. 151.

27. H. Werner and B. Kaplan, *Symbol Formation* (New York: John Wiley, 1963), p. 19.

28. J. Piaget, *Biology and Knowledge* (Edinburgh: Edinburgh University Press, 1971), pp. 35–37.

29. O. H. Mowrer, *Learning Theory and the Symbolic Processes* (New York: John Wiley and Sons, 1960), p. 277.

30. W. Penfield and L. Roberts, *Speech and Brain Mechanisms* (Princeton: Princeton University Press, 1959), p. 246.

31. *Ibid.*, p. 233.

32. *The Republic of Plato*, translated by A. Bloom (New York: Basic Books, 1968).

33. See the review of some Western conceptions of intuition by Malcolm Westcott in *Toward a Psychology of Intuition* (New York: Holt, Rinehart and Winston, 1968), pp. 1–22.

34. See article on Jung by Ruth L. Munroe in her *Schools of Psychoanalytic Thought* (New York: Dryden Press, 1955).

35. A. H. Maslow, *Toward a Psychology of Being* (New York: Van Nostrand, 1962), p. 67.

36. Monroe, *Schools of Psychoanalytic Thought*, p. 541.

37. This summary of Jung's basic theoretical concepts regarding consciousness is based on Jolande Jacobi, *The Psychology of C. G. Jung* (New Haven: Yale University Press, 1958), pp. 5–10.

38. *Ibid.*, p. 204.

39. *Ibid.*, p. 92.

40. *Ibid.*, p. 50.

41. C. G. Jung, "Approaching the Unconscious," in *Man and His Symbols*, edited by C. G. Jung (London: Aldus Books, 1964), p. 38.

42. *Vākyapadīya* I:123.

43. V. K. Chari, " 'Rasa' as an Aesthetic Concept: Some Comments from the Point of View of Western Criticism." Unpublished paper presented at the International Sanskrit Conference, New Delhi, March 1972, p. 7.

Selected Bibliography

Primary Sources

1. Works by Bhartṛhari

Nīti and Vairāgya Śatakas of Bhartṛhari. Sanskrit text with commentary and English translation by M. R. Kale. Delhi: Motilal Banarsidass, 1971.

Vairāgya-Śatakam of Bhartṛhari. Sanskrit text with English translated and edited by Swami Gambhirananda. Calcutta: Advaita Ashrama, 1963.

Vākyapadīya of Bhartṛhari with Commentary. English translation by K. A. Subramania Iyer. Poona: Deccan College, ch. I, 1965, and ch. III, pt. i, 1971.

2. Works by Other Ancient Sanskrit Scholars

Brahma-Sūtra-Śaṅkara-Bhyāṣya. English translation by V. M. Apte. Bombay: Popular Books Depot, 1960.

Dhvanyāloka of Anandavardhana. English translation by K. Krishnamoorthy. Poona: Oriental Book Agency, 1955.

Patañjali-Yogadarsanam. Varanasi: Bhāratīya Vidhyā Prakāśana, 1963.

Patañjali's Yoga Sūtras. With the commentary of Vyāsa and gloss of Vācaspati Miśra, translated by Rama Prasada. Allahabad: Bhuvaneswari Asrama, 1924. Best English translation.

Sarva-Darśana-Saṁgraha by Madhva. English translation by E. B. Cowell and A. E. Gough. Varanasi: Chowkamba Sanskrit Series Reprint, 1961.

Ślokavārtika by Kumārilabhāṭṭa. English translation by Ganganatha Jha. Calcutta: Asiatic Society of Bengal, 1909.

Sphoṭasiddhi of Maṇḍana Miśra. English translation by K. A. Subramania Iyer. Poona: Deccan College, 1966.

Secondary Sources

Chakrabarti, T. *Indian Aesthetics and Science of Language.* Calcutta: Sanskrit Pustak Bhandar, 1971.

Chakravarti, P. K. *The Linguistic Speculations of the Hindus.* Calcutta: University of Calcutta, 1933. A helpful general introduction to *sphoṭa* theory.

CHATTERJEE, S. *The Nyāya Theory of Knowledge.* Calcutta: University of Calcutta, 1965. Contains a good review of the approaches of the various Indian philosophical schools to language.

DATTA, D. M. *The Six Ways of Knowing.* Calcutta: University of Calcutta, 1960.

GHOSE, AUROBINDO. *On the Veda.* Pondicherry: Sri Aurobindo Ashram Press, 1956. First few pages contain an excellent English presentation of the orthodox Hindu view of the Vedas.

IYER, K. A. SUBRAMANIA. *Bhartṛhari: A Study of the Vākyapadīya in the Light of the Ancient Commentaries.* Poona: Deccan College, 1969. Without doubt the best single secondary source on the *Vākyapadīya.* Also has helpful general sections on Bhartṛhari's dates, works, and metaphysical background.

JHA, GANGANATHA. *Pūrva-Mīmāṁsā in Its Sources.* Varanasi: Banaras Hindu University, 1964.

KANE, P. V. *History of Sanskrit Poetics.* Delhi: Motilal Banarsidass, 1971.

KAVIRAJ, GOPINATH. "The Doctrine of Pratibhā in Indian Philosophy," *Annals of the Bhandarkar Oriental Research Institute,* 1924, pp. 1–18 and 113–32. Best English description of *pratibhā,* or supersensuous intuition.

LAHIRI, P. C. *Concepts of Rīti and Guṇa in Sanskrit Poetics.* Ramma: University of Dacca, 1937.

MURTI, T. R. V. *The Central Philosophy of Buddhism.* London: Allen and Unwin, 1960.

———. "Some Thoughts on the Indian Philosophy of Language." Presidential Address to the 37th Indian Philosophical Congress, 1963. Best overview of the approaches to language in Indian philosophy.

MURTY, K. S. *Revelation and Reason in Advaita Vedānta.* New York: Columbia University Press, 1959.

PANDEY, K. C. *Abhinavagupta.* Varanasi: Chowkhamba Sanskrit Series, 1963.

———. *Comparative Aesthetics,* vols I and II. Varanasi: Chowkhamba Sanskrit Series, 1959.

RAJA, K. KUNJUNNI. *Indian Theories of Meaning.* Adyar: Adyar Library, 1963.

SASTRI, GAURINATH. *The Philosophy of Word and Meaning.* Calcutta: Sanskrit College, 1959. A most helpful book for understanding Bhartṛhari's *Vākyapadīya.*

SANKARAN, A. *Some Aspects of Literary Criticism in Sanskrit.* Madras: University of Madras, 1929.

Glossary of Sanskrit Terms

abhidhā, primary meaning.
abhiniveśa, clinging to life.
abhyāsā, habitual steadying of the mind in Yogic concentration.
adhyāsā, superimposition.
āgama, scriptural truth, including *śruti*, *smṛti*, the epics and Purāṇas.
ahaṁkāra, ego.
ahimṣā, nonviolence in thought and deed.
akliṣṭa, unafflicted, pure, free from ignorance.
ālambana, supporting object, ground.
alaṁkāra, figure of speech.
antaḥkaraṇa, the internal mental organ composed of the *buddhi*, *ahaṃkāra*, and *manas* functions.
anumāna, inference.
aparigraha, absence of avarice.
apauruṣeya, used to indicate that Vedic scripture is authorless, eternal, and therefore safeguarded from error.
apūrva, special force or residual effect of a religious sacrificial act that inheres in the sacrificer as a special kind of potency until it brings the reward of heaven.
artha, word-meaning as distinct from word-sound; the inner meaning of a word; object.
āsana, Yogic posture for the purpose of immobilizing the body, e.g., lotus position.
asmitā, egoity.
asteya, nonstealing.
ātman, self or soul.
AUM, the sacred syllable of Hinduism that symbolizes and evokes all levels of consciousness, all knowledge of the Divine.
avidyā, the obscuring veil of human ignorance that, when removed, reveals knowledge of reality.

bhāṣya, commentary.
bīja, seed or seed state.
brahmacarya, celibacy in thought and action.
Brahman, the Absolute; the Divine; sometimes characterized as pure consciousness.
Brahma Sūtra, a summary and exposition of the basic teachings of the Upaniṣads from the viewpoint of the Vedānta school of philosophy. It is said to have been composed by Bādarāyaṇa about the second century B.C. Important commentaries on the *Brahma Sūtra* have been written by Śaṇkara and Ramanuja.
buddhi, the level of consciousness characterized by intelligent discrimination; intellect.
buddhitattva, pure collective or universal consciousness containing within it all intellects of individuals.

citta, consciousness including both the level of awareness and the level of unconsciousness.
citta vṛtti, a particular mental state.

darśana, viewpoint; philosophical school.
dhāraṇā, short Yogic concentration with momentary loss of subject-object duality.
dharma, one's religious and moral duty in life; doing one's *dharma* produces spiritual merit; also may mean truth.
dhvani, the physical sound or the uttered syllables of a word.
dhvani (in Indian aesthetics), the use of poetic or dramatic words to suggest or evoke a feeling that is too deep, intense, and universal to be spoken.
dhyāna, Yogic concentration lasting several *dhāraṇās*; the uninterrupted flow of fixed concentration upon an *artha*, or object.
dveṣa, disgust.

guṇa, a characteristic or quality; usually refers to the three *guṇas* of consciousness: *sattva*, *rajas*, and *tamas*.
guru, spiritual teacher.

Īśvara, in the Yoga view is the divine *guru* of the ancient *ṛṣis*; it is the Divine Word of the scripture in its transcendental essence that makes up the pure consciousness of Īśvara.
Īśvarapranidhana, offering up of all action and thought to the Lord Īśvara.

jīva, the empirical self, individual being.
jñāna, true, unobscured knowledge of the word or object.

kaivalya, the Saṅkhya term for release; the *puruṣa* fully revealed in its isolated splendor.

kārikā, a concise verse requiring an interpretative commentary for its understanding.

karma, the trace or seed left behind by each thought or action that predisposes one to a similar thought or action in the future.

kleśas, constantly changing painful states of consciousness.

kliṣṭa, afflicted by ignorance.

kratu, an energy (within the word) that seeks to burst forth into expression; the drive to diversity within the unitary whole, or *sphoṭa*.

lakṣaṇa, secondary meaning.

madhyamā vāk, language as thought that has not yet been uttered.

mahāvākyas, the great criterion sentences of the Upaniṣads, e.g.; "That thou art."

manas, the mental organ that collects and coordinates information.

mantra, a verse of poetic scripture in praise of the Divine.

māyā, the illusion of the manifold world, which is really only the unitary Absolute; for Śaṇkara, has the ontological status of being neither real nor unreal but inexpressible.

Mīmāṁsā, one of the six orthodox schools of Indian philosophy, argues for the authorlessness and eternality of the letter sounds of the Vedas.

mokṣa, release, freedom from the suffering and bondage of this world, oneness with the Divine.

nāda, physical sound.

nirvāṇa, Buddhist state of release or enlightenment.

nirvicāra, a pure form of *samādhi* in which the meaning or object is fully revealed in its very essence. No notions of time, space, or causality are present.

Nirvitarka, trance concentration upon the gross form of the object, but freed from the confusion of memory and the conventional use of words.

niyamas, positive Yogic practices for the purifying of body and mind.

Parama Śiva, Śiva as the Absolute Lord upon which the *parā vāk* of Kashmir is dependent.

parā vāk, an ultimate or fourth level of language developed by Kashmir Saiva writers.

paśyanti vāk, level of intuitive or flashlike understanding of the sentence meaning as a whole.

prajñā, direct intuitive knowledge of things as they are in themselves, rather than as they appear to us.

prakṛti, nonintelligent matter, one side of the Sāṇkhya-Yoga metaphysical duality.

pramā, true cognition or knowing as distinct from false knowing.

pramāṇa, a true or valid way of knowing, e.g.; perception. Although there is argument in Indian philosophy, six *pramāṇas* are often discussed: perception, inference, analogy, presumption, nonapprehension (*abhāva*), and the revelatory power of speech (*śabda*). It is with the *pramāṇa* of *śabda* that Bhartṛhari is most concerned.

prāṇa, breath; the instrumental cause of speech at the lower levels of language.

praṇava, AUM, the sacred "root" sound from which all language flows forth.

prāṇāyāma, regulation of respiration.

pratibhā, immediate supersensuous intuition; supernormal perception that transcends the ordinary categories of time, space, and causality, and has the capacity to directly "grasp" the real nature of things.

pratyāhāra, withdrawal of senses from worldly attachments.

pratyaya, ground or support in which the word-sound and word-meaning inhere.

puruṣa, an individual pure consciousness, one side of the Sāṅkhya-Yoga metaphysical duality.

rāga, passion.

rajas, the aspect of consciousness that is passion or energy.

rasa, a dominant mood evoked in the aesthetic experience of poetry and drama.

rasadhvani, the inner essence of the aesthetic experience that is beyond all conceptual expression.

rīti, poetic style.

ṛṣi, an original seer or "speaker" of Hindu scripture. One who has purged himself of all ignorance, rendering his consciousness transparent to the Divine Word.

śabda, word or words that when spoken convey knowledge — especially of the Divine.

Śabdabrahman, the Absolute, the Divine for Bhartṛhari; the intertwined unity of word and consciousness that is the one ultimate reality; for Bhartṛhari both the material and efficient cause of creation; also called the Divine Word, or *Daivī—Vāk*.

śabdapūrvayoga, the spiritual discipline of meditating upon the Divine Word, leads to *mokṣa*, or release.
Śabdatattva, Brahman as the omniscient word-principle.
sādhanā, a personal discipline or practice for spiritual self-realization.
samādhi, trance state of consciousness with no subject-object distinction.
samprajñāta samādhi, "seeded" or trance concentration upon an object, as opposed to "unseeded" or trance concentration without an object.
saṁsāra, rebirth in the suffering and bondage of this world; the continual round of birth-death-rebirth; the world of phenomena.
saṁskāra, a memory trace that has the dynamic quality of a seed that is constantly ready to sprout.
samtoṣa, contentment.
saṅketa, convention of language usage as maintained by the elders in this and previous generations.
Sāṅkhya, one of the six orthodox schools of Indian philosophy, argues for a dualism of matter (*prakṛti*) and individual souls (*puruṣas*).
śānta rasa, the aesthetic experience of spiritual serenity; the absolute *rasa* into which all other emotions subside.
śāstra, authoritative teaching.
sattva, the aspect of consciousness that is brightness or intelligence.
sattva saṁskāra, series, continuous flow of pure consciousness as it would be in the mind of the Lord (Īśvara); no distinction between word and meaning, but only the constant presence of meaning as a whole.
satya, truthfulness.
savicāra, a form of *samādhi* in which little error is present; the intensity of concentration produces transparent *sattva* so that the true meaning or object (*artha*) stands revealed with only slight distortions of time, space, and causality.
savitarka, indistinct Yogic concentration or *samādhi* in which memory, word, and object are indiscriminately mixed together.
sāyuja, the highest spiritual goal of union with the Divine.
smṛti, secondary scripture, that which has been remembered, e.g., *Bhagavad-Gīta*.
sphoṭa, a meaning-whole or idea that eternally exists within consciousness and that is evoked or manifested by the spoken words of sentences; can be directly perceived through intuition.
śruti, primary scripture; that which has been seen by the *ṛṣis*; includes the Vedic hymns, Brāhmaṇas, and Upaniṣads.
sthayibhavas, basic dominant moods inherent in every psyche at birth.
svādhāya, concentrated scriptural study including both meditation upon verses and chanting of AUM.

svarga, not the final release or goal of Hinduism, but the place where the fruits of the spiritual merit one has achieved are enjoyed; heaven.

tamas, the aspect of consciousness that is dullness or inertia.
tanmātras, subtle primary elements; inner counterparts to the gross sense experiences of sound, touch, color or shape, flavor, smell.
tapas, psychic heat or energy generated from the practice of austerities; bearing with equanimity the pairs of opposites such as heat and cold, hunger and thirst.

vāgyoga, Yoga or concentration upon speech.
vaikharī vāk, gross or physical level of uttered speech.
vairāgya, turning away of the mind from all forms of worldly attachment.
vāk, language that is thought of as having various levels — from the gross form of the spoken word to the subtle form of the highest intuition.
vākya sphoṭa, intuitive understanding or direct perception of the sentence meaning as a whole idea.
varṇa, letter sounds.
vāsanā, a habit pattern of thought and/or action; composed of reinforced *karmas*.
Vedānta, one of the six orthodox schools of Indian philosophy, often identified with the monistic absolutism of Śaṅkara.
Vedas, the primary Hindu scriptures including the early hymns, the Brāhmaṇas, and Upaniṣads. The Vedas are organized into four collections called *Ṛg*, *Sāma*, *Yajur*, and *Atharva*.
vikalpa, the mixing or superimposing of two or more mental states so that knowledge is obscured and error produced.
vṛtti, a commentary.
Vyākaraṇa, the Grammar school; one of the traditional schools of Indian philosophy; Patañjali and Bhartṛhari are among the leaders of this school.
vyañjanā, special suggestive function of poetic phrases.

yamas, Yogic practices of self-restraint, e.g., *ahimṣā*, or nonviolence.
Yoga, one of the six schools of orthodox Indian philosophy; describes a practical psychological discipline for achieving release; systematized by Patañjali.
yogāṅgas, steps or aids to the practice of Yoga.

Index

Abidhā, 84
Abhinavagupta, 49, *86–87*, 88, 91, 113
Abhiniveśa, 98, *99–100*
Abhyāsa, 73
Adhyāsa, 69, 132n36
Aesthetics, 81–94, 111, 114, 122
Āgama, 55, 56
Ahamkara, 61–64, 71, 72
Ahimṣā, 101
Alamkara, 86, 113
Anandavardhana: "Dhvanyāloka," 80, 84, 85, 86, 87, 113; "Abhinavabharatī," 86, 88
Antaḥkaraṇa, 64, 67, 72, 74, 75
Anumāna, 22, 71, 78, 87, 118
Aparigraha, 101
Apte, V. S., 35
Apūrva, 41–42
Archetype, 93, 94, 118, 120, 121, 122
Artha, 36, 50, 62–72, 76, 77, 82, 83, 84, 85, 88, 90, 91, 93, 113, 116, 118, 121
Āsana, 73, 75, 77, 101, 103
Asmitā, 58, 98, *99*
Asteya, 101
Ātman, 86, 103
AUM, 18, 22, 35, 36, 45, 56, 74, 102, 106
Aurobindo, 111
avidyā, 21, 26, 27, 57, 62, 68, 69, *98–99*, 107, 110

Beach, L. R., 94
Bergson, H., 118
Bhagavad Gītā, 108
Bharata, "Nātyaśāstra," 85, 88
Bhartṛhari: assumption of Yoga psychology, 54; conservative in religion, 17, 19; contributions to India, 105–14; date, 11, 95–96; heuristic levels of language, 78; means to mokṣa, 72–79; metaphysical background, 20; Mīmāṁsā versus, 23–24; poet, the, 95–98, 105, 111–12, 134n4; royal childhood, 16; śabda, his high view of, 21, 30; Saṅkara versus, 25

WORKS — POETRY:

"Niti Śataka," 95–97, 101
Śatakas, 15
"Sriñgāra Śataka," 96–97, 103
"Vairagya Śataka," 95, *96–104*, 112

WORKS — PROSE:

"Vākyapadīya," 15, 19, 20, *31–52*, 54, 56, 58, 59, 62, 65, 66, 69, 71, 78, 80, 81, 83, 95, 96, 106, 108–14, 131n15
"Vṛtti" on the "Vākyapadīya," 31, 50

Bīja, 55, 58
Biardeau, M., 128n2
Brahmacarya, 101
Brahman: 21, 101, 104, 108, 109, 110; as speech or *vāk*, 17, 30, 33, 35, 48, 50, 55, 56, 106, 108
Brāhmaṇas, 17, 21, 29
Buddha, 27, 28, 29
Buddhism, 20, *27–29*, 30, 31, 54, 105, 110, 114
Buddhi, 47, 61–69, 71
Buddhitattva, 61, 62, 63, 69, 72, 91, 93, 131n23